George F. Johnson

AND HIS INDUSTRIAL

DEMOCRACY

BY WILLIAM INGLIS

ILLUSTRATED

HUNTINGTON PRESS

New York

FIRST EDITION

PRINTED IN THE UNITED STATES OF AMERICA

BY H. WOLFF, NEW YORK

Printing Statement:

Due to the very old age and scarcity of this book,
many of the pages may be hard to read due to the
blurring of the original text, possible missing pages,
missing text and other issues beyond our control.

Because this is such an important and rare work, we
believe it is best to reproduce this book regardless of
its original condition.

Thank you for your understanding.

George F. Johnson

IT IS difficult to believe, especially in days of economic distress, that such a union of capital and labor as the Endicott Johnson Corporation and its workers actually exists. That employers and employees in a great industry have pulled together for nearly two generations without clashing, and thereby achieved a great success, is hard to conceive. Add to this that the chiefs of the enterprise live among their nineteen thousand workers in a harmonious family, a veritable industrial democracy, with homes, playgrounds, parks, libraries, hospitals and a fine medical service —and nine out of ten will call it a dream.

To gather facts about this phenomenon, I lived in the community for three months in the summer of 1934, studied the army of tanners and shoemakers at work, in their homes, in their churches and libraries, on their playing fields, at their festivals, in the clinics, hospitals and convalescent homes, on workdays, Sundays and holidays. (In this study I was aided by the officers and executives of the company, by many of the workers, and especially by Mr. Leo J. Callahan, editor of the Workers' Page, all of whom I thank.)

Soon I began to feel that, while the many good things I had heard of the organization were true, few outsiders would credit them. I still feel that many will doubt. But, happily, the whole business is open to anyone who wants to see.

While leaders of government and of industry have been trying, almost in despair, to find a way to reconcile labor and capital, George F. Johnson has not only found it but followed it for forty years. His inborn spirit of friendship and fair play has inspired in his people a coöperation which has produced comfort and happiness for them and prosperity for all concerned. There is no patent on the plan. Anyone who will may use it. And it has a virtue that commends it to all good business men—it pays.

WILLIAM INGLIS

Fieldston, New York City
February, 1935

CONTENTS

ILLUSTRATIONS

Decorated end-papers from a drawing by Georg Salter

George F. Johnson

AND HIS INDUSTRIAL

DEMOCRACY

CHAPTER ONE

Friendship and fair play—George F.'s background

ONE of the most extraordinary facts concerning the Endicott Johnson Corporation is its friendly relation with its workers. It has never had any labor trouble; and it employs nineteen thousand men and women who can make one hundred seventy-five thousand pairs of shoes each day. Its twenty-nine factories, surrounded by the homes, gardens, farms, parks and playgrounds of the workers, add to the attractiveness of the Susquehanna valley between Binghamton and Endicott, New York.

The workers have lived in comfort and happiness for four decades. They read in the newspapers about conflict between labor and capital, but it never touches them. Through the lean years of the great depression they have not suffered deprivation, and in the years of plenty they have prospered.

Meanwhile, through good times and bad, the Endicott Johnson Corporation has grown steadily greater and more successful.

Such a phenomenon as this challenges attention. If all American workers and employers lived on such terms as these people live, strife between labor and capital could not occur. It is not extravagant to believe that much of the poverty and suffering since 1929 would have been avoided if American industries had been conducted on the Endicott Johnson plan. Moreover, if American industry generally followed the principles established by George F. Johnson, it seems reasonable to suppose that we would thereby achieve a far greater degree of stability in our industrial order than we have ever had.

That is why for months I have studied this community, lived in it, felt it, talked with workers and chiefs of every degree, watched them at work and at play, visited them in their homes and—perhaps I flatter myself—made many friends among them.

I believe I have learned why these people have lived with one another for generations in harmony. It is because of two things: Friendship and fair play.

Each side of the industry understands the other— though it is hardly accurate to think of these employers and employees as two sides of the situation. They are really one group, from the chiefs to the newest apprentices, fellow workers, living next door to one another, working side by side, playing the same games, going to the same schools, worshipping in the

*Birthplace of George F. Johnson at
Milford, Massachusetts*

*Mount Hollis Seminary at Holliston, Massachusetts, where
George F. Johnson finished his schooling at the age of thirteen*

his brother, C. Fred., then by his own and C. Fred.'s sons getting into the harness, and now, as has been said, by the incoming third generation—but George F. is the man who originated the system, developed it and carried it forward, often against tough opposition. Let us try to see what makes him what he is and what he does.

George Francis Johnson was born in the town of Milford, Massachusetts, October 14, 1857. His father, Francis A. Johnson, native of Franklin, near by, came of generations of hardy sailors and farmers, who lived in and near Plymouth. After a whaling cruise and a few other voyages, he came ashore, learned the trade of making and treeing boots. He married Sarah Jane Aldrich, of an old New England family, a gentle soul, beloved by her neighbors for her many acts of kindness. Their children were Oscar, C. Fred., George F., Harry L., and Charlotte.

Little George was in his fourth year when the Confederates fired on Fort Sumter. His father led one hundred men to the recruiting post at Milford and marched off to the war as a lieutenant, soon to be made a captain. Mrs. Johnson took her three boys to the depot to see him off, though George was too young to remember it. After the war the captain commanded Fort Wentworth in Boston Harbor for a year, then went back to his boot-treeing. That is, he stretched the new boots on snug-fitting trees, rubbed dressing into them and gave them a smart, trim look that helped to sell them.

A fiery, blue-eyed, red-bearded giant, Captain Johnson worked with tremendous energy, seldom stayed in one town for more than one year, because he was always finding a better job somewhere else, tried his hand at anything that promised more profit. Little George, like his brothers, had to work hard from the time he was old enough to get about alone. He did not like study, but he liked to play ball after school. He was a crack pitcher, and the boys made him captain of the nine. The instinct for leadership appeared early—when as a child he played horse, he was always the driver, never the horse. His mother was a devout Methodist; so George attended church and Sunday school regularly, though not with enthusiasm.

The boys had no playground but the streets, and if by chance they broke a window they had to dodge through alleys for days and hide in the woods, in fear of the police. There was no such thing as "the old swimmin' hole" for them. George learned to swim in a muddy pool in a cow pasture, long since dried up. Far away was an old mill pond about fifty feet wide. Any boy who could swim across that was a hero. Because he hadn't a fair chance as a youngster is one reason why George F. Johnson has given so many ball fields and playgrounds and swimming

pools to the boys and girls in the valley of the Susquehanna.

In the few years he had lived George had already
gained valuable experience. Hard work and hard
knocks were nothing new to him. When his father
kept the Winthrop House at Holliston, nine-year-
old George was busy after school piling wood to feed
the airtight stoves that heated the bedrooms. For this
his father paid him fifteen cents a week. Lugging
armfuls of jagged sticks from the cellar to the third
or fourth floor grew tiresome; so he hired boys to do
it for him, and gave them marbles for pay. He was
a crack shot at marbles, and he always had a lot on
hand.

He was a born trader. Between breakfast and
school one of his chores was to carry eggs to the
store and swap them for groceries: he always washed
the eggs, so that they looked their best and fetched
a good price. With his brother Fred, four years older,
he clipped pictures from Harper's Weekly and the
Police Gazette that guests left in their rooms, and
pasted them on rolls of paper. They wound these
strips on spindles and unwound them across a screen
under red and blue lights, down in the basement.
They called it a "puppy" show, meaning a puppet
show. Neighbor boys crowded in to see these primitive movies, and each paid ten pins admission. Fred
and George sold the pins to their mother, a hundred
for a cent.

Fred was jolly and a good mixer, helped in the dining room and ate there. George hated to dress up; he did the rough chores and ate in the buttery or out in the kitchen with the help, who did not care how he dressed. He worked as hard as anyone else, but he never stopped studying how to do things better and with less labor—hasn't stopped that study yet, by the way. At supper one Friday Captain Johnson told George to whitewash the back fence, and he'd pay him ten cents for the job. George went out to see four boys who played ball on his team.

There were only two brushes; so when the four boys came round next morning George worked each boy fast for a spell, then let the next boy take the brush and try to work faster. He mixed the whitewash in two buckets, and watched to make sure none was splashed and that all the fence was evenly covered.. In less than two hours the job was done and paid for. George gave each boy one cent, according to contract, and with the remaining half dime bought a bag of candy, which he shared with the four, a bonus they didn't expect. It was his first experience as a leader of industry. When I asked Mr. Johnson about the incident the other day, he said, "It's true, but it sounds too much like Tom Sawyer."

It happened in 1867, long before Mark Twain wrote Tom Sawyer.

George always shared his apples or candy with his gang, had as keen an instinct for giving as he had for trading. "Seems almost like yesterday," says his brother Fred, "that I was down cellar, holding a kerosene lamp while George was cutting up a hog he had raised and butchered. As he cut it up, he'd say, 'This is for the Soandsos,' or 'I guess I'll give this rack of chops to Soandso.' Looked as if he couldn't enjoy it unless his friends had some, too."

That instinct for helping and giving, the boys inherited from their mother—and they often saw her act on it. When the supper dishes were dried and put away, after a long day taking care of her boys and her home, Mrs. Johnson would throw a wrap over her shoulders and open the door.

"Where are you going, Jane?" her husband would ask.

"Why, Mrs. Stephens is sick," Mrs. Johnson would reply, "and I'm going to sit with her a little while." Many a time, when a sick woman needed constant care, her little while would grow into an all night session; but the wife and mother came home cheerful as ever and went about her daily routine as if nothing out of the way had happened. She did not talk about the duty of helping people: she did it. Long afterward George F. reminded his brother Fred of these incidents.

"While we may credit our energy to Father," he wrote, "we surely must feel that the good impulses we find in ourselves are our heritage from Mother."

CHAPTER TWO

George F.'s boyhood—He rises in his trade

A HUSKY, blue-eyed, red-haired boy of thirteen came briskly up the street toward an ugly old wooden house in Ashland, Massachusetts, at seven o'clock of a bright June morning in 1870. It was one of the factories of Seaver Brothers, in the heart of the boot-making district of America, and in it the boy was to begin to learn the trade.

He stared gloomily at the ugly house, for he liked play far better than work; but his father had spoken, and he knew what he had to do. So he walked rapidly to the side entry, down four stone steps and into the grimy cellar, dimly lighted by four windows heavily coated with dust. A dozen lads, about his own age, were going to work in the gloom.

"You Captain Frank Johnson's boy?" the foreman asked him.

"Yes; I'm George F.," the lad answered. The man wrote his name and the date in a book, led him to a

Winthrop House at Holliston, Massachusetts, about 1866. This inn was in the charge of Captain Francis A. Johnson. His sons, C. Fred, aged eleven years, and George F., aged nine years, worked here

chopping block beside a pile of dirt-caked and wrinkled old boots and handed him a hatchet.

"Put your lunch basket on the ledge," he said; "chop the soles and heels off these boots, same as these other fellows. Keep at it fast as you can, but be sure you don't slit the upper part. We want to use every bit of this leather."

George was used to handling tools, and he soon learned the art of chopping true along the line of pegs that fastened on the boot-sole. He cut the heel free, got a grip on the sole, and ripped it off. Sometimes it held fast, and the splintered pegs tore his fingers; but he chopped away, and soon had as big a pile of bootlegs as any of the others.

Young Johnson had not been eager to learn boot-making. That was the chief industry of the region, and when he grew tired of school after seven years, during which his mind was much more on swimming, running and baseball than on study, his father told him he'd better find a job. He thought a while of going to sea, as his father had done long ago, but a three years' whaling cruise looked pretty dismal, so he took to the shop.

Bootmaking was the art George hoped to learn some day, but just now he was very uncomfortable. He did not cut his fingers much, and the work was not too hard, but it was monotonous and suffocating. As he chopped he shrank back as far as he could from the old boots without spoiling his aim with the hatchet, for the ancient leather gave out a fierce stench. From farmers, junk men bought old boots saturated with barnyard muck, and piled them in heaps, as they pile old rubber tires today. These stacks of old boots could be dried, cut, cleansed and made into smaller sizes; so manufacturers bought them by the ton.

The Seavers' cellar was twenty feet long and sixteen wide, not a big room, but after the boys had been at work half an hour they could not see clearly half its length. Dust. As the boys chopped and wrenched off soles, slit the long seams and pulled the bootlegs wide open, dust puffed out of the leather and hung about the cellar in clouds.

The young apprentice was reminded of the Black Hole of Calcutta—except that the lucky prisoners who died there did not suffer the torture of blinding, choking dust. He wanted to throw down the hatchet and break out—run anywhere to get a breath of good fresh air. But there was in his make-up a strong streak of the iron of New England, the persistence that had tamed the forest and dared the seas, and besides there was the Yankee shrewdness which taught him that he must work if he would eat. And if he must work, he might as well go ahead at this tough task in the hope of making something worth while out of it.

In the Seavers' cellar George was earning three dollars a week for six days' work, ten hours a day. His father had often toiled twelve hours a day in a factory; so the boy did not mind ten hours so much—and three dollars were three dollars. That was worth the struggle, and he knew the need of fighting for what you wanted. He had learned that at Marlboro.

Captain Johnson heard that the bowling alley over there was closed because the hardy bootmakers of the village wrecked it with their rioting. So no one could run it, eh? Well, he knew he could. He leased the alley, and took Fred and George along to set up the pins. They walked four miles to Marlboro Monday mornings and walked home late Saturday nights.

Teams hot from rolling the balls would cool off on beer and conversation. Presently they'd begin to lament the wrongs of old Ireland. "They'll be at it pretty soon," Captain Johnson would say. "Boys, hide the pins." Then some patriot would back his words with a blow, and the fists would fly fast—Fred and George standing by to enjoy the fine battle. Father and his bartender, bigger than he was, would open the front door and throw the warriors out.

When he had tossed the last one into the heap on the street, Captain Johnson would smile at the crowd and say: "Boys, you ought to be ashamed. Come in and have a beer on the house." They came, they had their beer, and they were very agreeable. No ill feeling. The captain was so happy in keeping the peace that he ran the bowling alley for months.

Another thing that reconciled George to the boot-chopping job was the regular pay. The Seavers did not cheat him as did old man Mellin, a devout heel-baller and edge-stoner on stogy boots. After a lot of smooth, friendly talk, he sold the boy a setting Brahma hen for a dollar and a quarter, sight unseen. As he pocketed the money, he said he liked to see a bright boy do well, and if that good, steady hen had her usual luck she'd hatch a brood of chicks that'd fetch a nice profit. When they went into the barn the hen was off the nest, clucking to thirteen plump, healthy little Brahmas.

The sight was too much for Mellin. "Here's your money, boy," he said, thrusting the payment into George's hand. "You'd best be getting along home now."

"Mellin's the meanest man I ever knew," George told Fred that night.

Bad as the work in the cellar was, it paid better than wood-chopping: George had earned two dollars at that a while before, walking six miles every day to and from the woods for two weeks. Boot-chopping paid three times as well as that. One day the boy poked his hand deep into an old mummy of a boot he was going to open, and found something hidden away up in the toe. He drew it out—a big bit of paper, wadded tight and dry as the boot itself. Carefully unrolling it, he saw as the dirt flaked off that the paper was green and had a figure 2 printed on each corner.

"Hey!" he called to the boy at the next block. "Look! I've found a two-dollar bill!"

"Here—what's this?" cried a harsh voice over his shoulder, and the strong hand of boss Gardiner reached down and grabbed the money. "Boy," he said, "don't you know everything that comes in here belongs to me?"

The boss jammed the bill in his pocket—and George Johnson got a job in another shop just as soon as he could. He did not waste breath in complaining to the Seavers, but he thought of Gardiner's meanness for years. At the moment it was only one more of the hardships that a poor boy of the shoe towns had to suffer in silence; yet perhaps his resentment of this injustice inspired in George F. that devotion to the Square Deal which has always been the rule in his factories.

There were boot factories in all the towns for miles around, and George got a job at "bottoming" boots, as they called it—fastening on the welts and soles— and at "heel-balling." Farmers took home a dozen pairs at a time for their families to finish, and George worked in a big shop. He had a passion for efficiency, and he constantly studied how to do the job better and in an easier way. After two years' experience, the fifteen-year-old lad wanted to hire three or four men and run a bottoming room and be his own boss. He was sure he could run a room successfully.

His craving for sport was constant, too, and wherever he worked he got together a baseball team, which he usually called the Pioneers. He was pitcher and captain; not that he asked for it, but the others seemed to expect him to lead. The nines had lively matches Saturday afternoons, shop against shop, with a keg of beer on third base. Underhand pitching was the rule, so that there was a great deal of hitting and running—raising such a thirst that after a few innings the batters dashed straight to third on every hit. Then came protests, hot arguments and a lively scrap.

Nobody was hurt much, and there were no grudges. In this mixture of hard work and hard play young Johnson grew big and speedy—and played such good ball that he often earned five dollars for pitching a game. Made a litle money promoting boxing matches, too, and once had the honor of shaking hands with John L. Sullivan, whom he admired for his honesty and efficiency.

When he was sixteen, Johnson heard that they needed a good boot-treer in a factory at Worcester. He had not much money, but his little brother Harry lent him twenty cents, all he had in his toy bank. George walked four miles to the railroad station at Ashland, talked with the ticket agent; then came out and stared hopelessly at the train.

"What's the matter, bub?" a fat passenger asked from an open window. "You sick?"

"No," said George F. "I've got a job at Worcester, but the fare is sixty-five cents, and all I have is sixty."

"Here you are, young man," said the passenger, handing down a nickel with a lordly flourish.

He was the only human being that ever gave George F. Johnson any money.

From one boot town to another the boy removed, earning bigger pay at every change. Soon he found that he could do his work faster than the others because he had a knack for it. He learned more and more about the trade, invented a better treeing mixture, and in a short time he was a first class boottreer at four dollars a day—top wages in those times. At seventeen he was working for Emery at Plymouth and at twenty-one he was boss of a treeing room, with thirty-five men under him. Emery thought he was too young, and turned him out. He quickly got another job. He made friends. His men liked him.

In the shops reckless piece workers could not wait for pay day, wanted their money right away. Some keen fellows at the bench who had saved money would buy their piece work coupons for half their face value. If young Johnson had a bit saved and a man needed money, he'd buy the man's coupons at their face value, never a penny less. Bosses were hard drivers, tyrants. George went into Coburn's shop, in Hopkinton, where he used to work, and was talking with a friend.

"I don't allow anyone to talk to my men," said Coburn, as he took George by the scruff of the neck and the slack of the pants and rushed him out to the street. Nothing uncommon about that. Workers generally spoke of the boss as "that —!"

After the Civil War men got tired of wearing a leg full of leather up to their knees, and began to buy shoes. Their demands called for a radical change in manufacturing methods and machinery. But the boot business had come into the hands of the younger generation, softly reared, easy livers, who thought they had a good thing and didn't pay much attention to it. They hated change, and before they woke up the shoe trade had passed them by, and they failed. But that was not the reason George F. Johnson left New England. He had married, and he needed more money. In Plymouth he wanted to buy a little home for $400, and hadn't forty dollars for first payment on it. Many a time since he has looked at it and called it "the big disappointment of my life." Besides, he was ambitious; wanted to take charge of more men. He left Plymouth to work for the Johnson Shoe Company at Milford—not relatives.

Coburn's Boot Factory at Hopkinton, Massachusetts. This is the factory from which the owner ejected young George F. Johnson because he had talked with one of the workers

A popular noon-time diversion in the E.J. factories—pitching quoits

CHAPTER THREE

Lestershire—George F. takes charge of the treeing room—Henry B. Endicott puts George F. in charge of the business

ONE Saturday morning in 1881 George F. Johnson received a letter that gave him a pleasant shock. It was from Joseph Diment, superintendent, asking him to come on at once and take charge of a treeing room in Lester Brothers' factory, in Binghamton. Addressed to "Mr. Johnson, Plymouth," his father had forwarded it to him at Milford. All that the youth knew about Binghamton was that it had a fine baseball team called the Crickets. But here was the chance for that better job of his dreams, to direct a bigger crew of workers. He had no money; so on Sunday he walked seven miles to Ashland, where he borrowed ten dollars from his brother Fred—which he had laid by for his winter's coal—walked seven miles home, and started for the new job.

As he slept in the steerage of the boat from Stonington, Connecticut, to New York, someone stole the collar and tie he had laid off. Tuesday morning he arrived in Binghamton. Without collar or cravat about his sturdy neck, he called on Diment and said he was ready to go to work.

The superintendent looked at the blue-eyed, ruddy-cheeked youth, nearly six feet tall, his old coat stretched tight over bulging muscles. There was an air of calm self-reliance about him—but he seemed very young—too young to boss a crowd of expert workers.

"I sent that letter to a man, not a boy," said Diment, puzzled. "Wait a minute. Send Spofford here." When Spofford came in Diment asked, "Is this the Johnson you said is a good boss treer?"

"No," said Spofford. "He's a man about my age, forty-eight or so."

"I'm that Johnson's son," said George F., "and I'm a first class boss. Give me a chance. You'll find that I can run a treeing room."

He did not know that his whole future hung on the next few seconds. What he knew too well was that he had just eight cents in the world and no way to get back home; that he had his family to keep, and that he must have this job. But he kept a stiff upper lip. As Diment hesitated, the look of quiet confidence in Johnson's eyes convinced him. "All right," he said.

In the factory dressing room next morning George F. was buttoning on a long linen duster, such as all foremen wore. "Hoh!" said a brawny Irishman next to him. "Are you going to tree boots in that thing?"

"No," said Johnson. "In that thing I'm going to have boots treed."

"All right, then, and good luck t' ye," said the Irishman. He and the other treers took a liking to the friendly new foreman, and under him they began to turn out more work and better work than any other crew in the house. It was an old shop, founded long ago by George and Horace Lester. George was re-tired, sick; Horace was dead, and his son, G. Harry, ran the business. He was a college man who had lived abroad, was a connoisseur of art and pleasant living; he had come into the business from the top and was not too familiar with details. At the moment he was about to buy ten thousand dollars' worth of wooden lasts, to make pegged shoes.

"Knock the iron sheathing off those lasts you've been using to make nailed shoes," young Johnson advised him; "use the wooden lasts that are left for your pegged shoes, and you'll save that expense." Mr. Lester saw the point and saved his money; so now and then he would ask the new foreman's opinion on problems as they arose.

When the factory needed more room, in 1888, Mr. Lester told George F. he thought he'd have to buy a lot across the street.

"Why don't you go down the river a few miles, buy farm land and build your factory there?" Johnson asked. "Then the workers can buy lots and build their homes near the shop."

This suggestion put in motion the train of events that led to the erection of the new Lester factory two miles down the Susquehanna valley from Binghamton; to the building of workers' homes around it; and at last to the astounding development of eight miles of factories and homes. Moreover, it was the beginning, or at least one of the beginnings, of the movement to take factory workers out of the crowded cities to live on the land, where they could escape the slums and lead decent, human lives.

This was one of the very first successful efforts to solve the problems of de-centralization and de-urbanization of industry with which industrialists and sociologists are now concerned. What these expert thinkers have tried to demonstrate with the aid of calculations and charts and graphs, this young shoemaker actually began in 1888, and has lived to carry out to an extent without parallel. I asked Mr. Johnson where he got the idea.

"I can't tell you," he said, "how the idea came to me; but it was there, a strong impulse, something I wanted to see done. You ask, did I read it? If I did, I can't remember ever reading it—no, nor of hearing it suggested.

"From the time I was twenty years old—yes, from

the time I was eighteen—my picture of a real factory was the shop out in the open country, with the homes of the workers around it in a little village. Then the men and their families could have gardens, could get fresh air and the sun, and bring up their children decently, away from the crowded city. I had thought of it for years, hoped to see it established; and after I had talked it out with Harry Lester he agreed with me.

"But he didn't follow my plan. He bought plenty of land, built his factory, and sold building lots to his workers at a profit. That was just the opposite to what I wanted; for my idea was to have the workers happy and comfortable in homes they could put up for little money. But Lester saw his chance to make quick money, and took it. I still believed in my plan —though I did not get a chance to put it through for years. And when I did, I had to fight for it. I was born fighting; I've had to fight for my ideas all my life, and I guess I'll die fighting.

"The trouble with most employers is that they don't see far enough ahead. If they did, if they had real vision, they'd see that they would be better off paying good wages and helping their workers to lead normal, happy lives, owning their homes and being a real part of the community. But the short-sighted employers want to make quick money, and think they can get it by paying as little as possible, exploiting their workers and the people who buy their product.

"Out in the West now there is a concern operating on a plan exactly the opposite to ours. They have their factories far apart; they cut wages down as far as they can, and they figure that when they have labor trouble in one plant they can close it down and do the work elsewhere. Foolish. They can't last and win through on that program. The Square Deal is the only one that pays in the long run.

"Every improvement we have made in the business since I've had charge of it has been my idea. That is not boasting: it is the simple truth, and I am telling you so that you can get the record right. It took me five years to persuade Endicott that we ought to tan our own leather. He asked, 'What do you know about tanning leather?' and I said, 'Money will hire men who will tan it.' I wanted to get away from paying the profits that are taken out at every step from hides to shoes, to cut out all unnecessary costs and pass the savings along to our workers, to our customers and our stockholders."

All this is a little ahead of the story, but it is worth telling here, to show the ideals that inspired young Johnson long before he came to Binghamton, and led to the development of a system of factories, homes, medical care, parks and playgrounds unique in industrial history—with workers' wages from twenty to thirty per cent higher than the rates prevailing elsewhere in the shoe industry. Years were to pass before these things were accomplished, but

George F. always had in mind his dream of building a community of happy and successful shoemakers.

Workers in the new factory came down from Binghamton in horse-cars to the city line. The Lester company chartered cars and made young Johnson conductor of one of them, without extra pay, of course. From the edge of town the workers had to walk a mile or so through plowed fields that turned to bogs after a rain. The new factory was a wooden structure, four hundred feet long and fifty feet deep, four stories high. At the suggestion of George F., who was now assistant superintendent as well as foreman of a room, they called it the Pioneer—which recalled the hustling ball team he used to lead. He worked as hard as anyone, perhaps a little harder, and often stopped at a bench to show a man how to improve. Among the many homes built by the Pioneer workers, he put up a little white house around the corner from the factory. He knew by bitter experience the trials and suffering of bringing up a family on scanty earnings—and he never forgot that experience. Fifty years have passed since he lived in that cottage, but he still keeps it neat and freshly painted.

Anxious faces stared out of the Pioneer windows one June afternoon when black clouds rolled up the western sky, backed down from the northward, turning day into night, and let loose floods of rain. As the thunder crashed and jagged yellow flashes darted through the gloom, the workers dodged away from their machines, afraid of being struck. A blast of tornado strength shook the building and heaved up its northern front like the side of a storm-tossed ship. "Out! All hands out for your lives!" George F. shouted.

"First thing I remember," an old-timer told me, "I found myself out in the street, in the middle of a puddle, pulling on my rubbers. In all that gale and cloudburst and lightning, George F. and Joe Diment lashed fast a set of ropes that held down the front of the factory. 'You can go in now,' George F. told us. 'The shop is solider than ever.' Seemed as if he always knew what to do."

There was a great deal to be done; for G. Harry Lester, having made a great deal of money selling land to his workers, had formed a real estate company, with investments in Yonkers and elsewhere, and told Diment to run the boot and shoe making while he was busy getting rich in real estate. Lack of foresight and planning let the factory stand idle at times, while at intervals all the four hundred workers were rushed at their utmost speed. Mr. Lester formed the Lester Boot & Shoe Company as a jobbing house to distribute the product of his Lestershire Manufacturing Company, in which Henry B. Endicott of Boston and other jobbers joined; but his real interest was in land speculation. Mr. Endicott put $10,000 into stock of the manufacturing company, which had

$150,000 capital, and he became the treasurer. He also lent money to the company in bad years, and took more stock as security.

The Lester enterprises prospered for a time, but in the depression of the 1890's bad years came oftener, with more borrowings from Mr. Endicott. The factory was making a thousand pairs of boots and work shoes a day—when it was operating—and had been doing a business of $600,000 a year. At last the lender came down to try to protect his interest. He had advanced a great deal of leather on credit, and it would pay better to make it up than to ship it back to Boston to be sold at second hand. He was already the largest stockholder, and he bought out all the others, including G. Harry Lester, who had lost in his speculations. The old chief and the new consulted on the problem of finding a new superintendent for the business. Mr. Endicott thought he could bring an expert from some New England factory, a man with a record for success in management.

"Why don't you take Johnson?" said Lester. "He wants to try it, and he has ideas. He's a treeing boss, and the workers are his friends. They'd do wonders for him."

"A man from the bench to run the whole business?" Mr. Endicott asked. "Let's see him."

"Young man," said Mr. Endicott when the young foreman came into the office, "how would you put this business on its feet?"

"I'd offer the workers an incentive to produce more goods by putting them on piece work," said Johnson, "and I'd cut out all the frills and unnecessary costs. We can save on material and in selling—save in lots of ways. Let me run the factory a year, and I'll show you how we can make better shoes for less money. You needn't pay me more than I'm getting now."

"We'll try it," said Mr. Endicott.

A new era in the shoe industry had begun.

CHAPTER FOUR

A new era in the shoe industry—Rapid growth
of the business under George F.'s manage-
ment—George F. becomes a partner
of Henry B. Endicott

T HE most striking thing about the new era was
the friendly spirit all through the factory. Joseph
Diment was a good superintendent, a hard worker,
fair to his men, faithful in carrying out the orders
of his chief. But he had learned his trade in England,
where no one is ever allowed to forget the difference
between master and servant, between class and class.
When young Johnson became his assistant, he told
him not to overlook the fact that Mr. Lester was the
master and that they two were deputy masters under
him: the workers must do as they were told, and no
nonsense about it—"We give orders, and they obey."

But George F. had a different background, a different feeling about his relations with the men. He
thought of the workers as friends—not of labor as

a commodity. His instinct for friendship was as strong as his gift for leadership. From his school days he had run his ball nines by playing the game better than the others and by his love of team work, based on a warm friendship for his companions. This was born in him, not a matter of policy or calculation. So was his impulse to share with his mates.

When he began as foreman in the Lester shop, these ideas still governed him, and he soon won many friends. They spoke the same language. His men were Jim and Bill and Tom and he was George F.— all fellow workers, doing the best they could for themselves and their families. He had no time to play ball now, but he was still one of the crowd, joined them in their frolics and mourned with those in distress. He was a real neighbor.

And when he took hold of the job of putting the Pioneer factory on its feet, he went at it without any fuss and feathers. "We have the chance of our lives now, if we go at it right," he told one and another as he busied himself about the shop—no speech-making, but a few words with friends here and there: "This concern can make money and give us steady work, so that we can keep our little homes and make a decent living; but it all depends on you and me. The first thing we'll do is to put all hands on piece work, so that every fellow who puts the best he has into his work can earn good wages. The soft-enders and clock-watchers won't do so well. The more good shoes you turn out, the better off you'll be."

The workers were well pleased with the new policy of the shop, which offered them a premium for industry. They turned to with such energy that all the leather on hand was quickly made up and sold as boots and shoes. Mr. Endicott sent down more orders and more leather, and the business rallied, began to flourish—while the new superintendent still drew only a foreman's pay, and studied every element of costs as if the business belonged to him.

When Mr. Endicott found that the improvement was keeping up, he visited Lestershire.

"Have you found any new way of making money?" he asked.

"I have," said George F. "It's costing us too much to sell our shoes—two men at four thousand a year each. I can save that eight thousand dollars."

"How?"

"By selling the boots and shoes myself."

"But you don't know anything about selling."

"I know our shoes better than any salesman does, and I can tell the buyers what's in them, why they're the best in the market—all about them."

Mr. Endicott let the salesmen go, and George F. went on the road. He wasted no time on mere hired buyers; saw no one but the heads of firms. He told them so convincingly of the stout leather and first-class workmanship in his shoes, how much better off they'd be by selling them, that he sold more shoes than the two salesmen. By going direct to the head men he saved time, and actually covered more territory than his predecessors.

Mr. Endicott was so delighted with the saving of the money and the greater business his new superintendent brought in that he came to Lestershire and asked George F. how much more he thought he ought to be paid.

"Nothing more just yet," said the ambitious young man. "We're experimenting now. Let's wait till we see how the business grows."

He had in mind a plan which he was certain must win success. When that was assured, he was going to risk his future on one bold stroke; and he would not fritter away his chances by considering small advances in pay. He was intent on the principles which were bound to win in the long run, and they were the chief concern.

"Just what were you aiming at when you refused higher wages after the business began to improve?" I asked him the other day.

"I believed," George F. replied, "that we could build up a great enterprise by making our workers comfortable, free of worry, whether in the factory or in their homes; by thinking of them and treating them as human beings, not machines to be run till they broke down and had to be scrapped; to make them as contented as we could within reason. Men everywhere respond to that kind of treatment. It is decent; it is common sense—and it pays, too; pays everybody in the enterprise and the whole community.

"We had all suffered from idle periods in the factory. Steady work at decent wages is better than a high wage scale with long lay-offs in dull times. I tried to arrange our business to run all through the year. Also we cut out every item of excessive cost by wiping out the middle men wherever we could. We never stopped looking for better methods. Any man with a new invention to make shoes better and cheaper didn't have to look for us—I was looking for him.

"I believed then, and I believe now, that a man is entitled to all he can make with his skill and his industry. He ought not to be held back by getting no more pay than shirkers or incompetents. Time wages slow a man down: he thinks of the end of his day's work, not of the beginning and doing the best he can.

"I've always wanted to share with our workers what we earn together. Mere money has no brains, no part in the management. All it is entitled to is security and a fair interest on the investment.

"I've always had in mind that picture of what a real factory should be—the factory in the country, with the comfortable homes of the workers around it. And it seems to me—always has seemed—that an employer ought to do everything he can to keep his workers well and happy. That's true Christianity. What do we read in Scripture? Christ went about *doing* good. Our business is Christianity in action."

An incident that happened not very long before George F. Johnson took charge of the Pioneer factory throws a light on his attitude toward all workers. Among letters from old citizens to the Chamber of Commerce, incidental to the centennial celebration of Binghamton, was one from an old lady, telling that Mr. Johnson gave her a baby carriage when he was a foreman in the Lester shop in that city. I chanced to see the letter, and called at her home. I found a tiny gray woman washing dishes. Her tired old eyes lighted up when I asked her about the gift.

"It's odd," she said, "but I remember what Mr. Johnson did for me so much better than I remember the man himself. I'm nearly eighty-one; so my memory's none too good. You see, my husband had run off with another woman and left me with three small children. I had to do something to feed those little mouths, so I took in washing. Mr. Johnson lived in Mill Street, two blocks from me, and he used to bring their washing. When he called for it one Saturday, he saw little Emmy, eighteen months old, and asked me if I had a baby carriage. I said no. He said they had just got a new carriage and he'd give me the old one. I said that would be a blessing, and on Monday when he brought the wash he was pushing

Seaver & Sons' Factory at Ashland, Massachusetts, where George F. Johnson won his first promotion

it in the carriage. So my oldest could take care of baby Emmy and give me more time to wash. You see Mr. Johnson didn't wait till he was rich before he began to help working folks."

And here is another instance of George F.'s thought for others. Within a year after he was made superintendent of Pioneer, he moved to a house some miles down Riverside Drive. He bought a horse, buggy, harness, laprobe and whip for eighty dollars, so he could drive to work. He had to save every possible minute to devote to the needs of the business —but he felt so embarrassed by his eighty dollars' worth of luxury while his comrades had to walk to work that he never drove up to the factory door. Instead, he stopped the horse between a haystack and a little knoll, out of sight of the factory, and walked to the door. After the six o'clock whistle, he walked to the haystack, where his wife was waiting to drive him home.

Quick sympathy and fair dealing with his neighbors, the workers, had much to do with George F. Johnson's success in reviving Mr. Endicott's Lester Boot and Shoe Company, but they were not all. He was a born trader, and the economies forced on him by his rugged New England upbringing had become second nature. He let nothing go to waste. He was constantly devising new ways to make shoes better and faster. When he showed them to his workers,

they were eager to follow the lead of their friend.
The business became more profitable every day.

Work in the Pioneer factory moved with a speed
and precision never known before. From the oldest
experts at the bench to the youngest apprentices, all
hands were keen to do their best, took a new interest
in turning out a better product and more of it. Not
for money alone—at least, not for mere piling up of
more pay coupons immediately. They were a crew
keyed up to racing pitch. What they were all aiming
at was to improve their methods so much that they
would excel any other outfit in the trade. This did
not happen by chance: their leader had set fire to
their imagination.

"We've got to make all we can *of* this concern, not
try to take all we can *out* of it," George F. told his
companions, as he watched them at their work day
by day. This was exactly opposite to the policy that
commonly prevailed in industry—to wring all that
was possible out of a shop, whether in profits or in
wages, with capital and labor fighting for the lion's
share. From the time that young Johnson, at the age
of fifteen, grew ambitious to run a shop, his ruling
idea had been to develop it for all it was worth, and
now that he had complete charge of the Lester factory he put it in operation. And, thanks to his friendship with the workers and their belief in him, he was
able to secure their enthusiastic support.

He had another controlling idea: the rock upon

which he built his whole business structure was to make better shoes for less money. To do this, he cut out elaborate methods, unnecessary operations—everything in the nature of frills. Once the people who sold the shoes and the people who wore them found out they were getting more for their money, the business was sure to grow—and nothing could stop it, so long as the correct principles were at work. With a steady stream of orders flowing in, employment and wages would be sure and steady—not the succession of rush seasons and long lay-offs that had been the rule for years.

Time soon proved the theory right. So many orders for shoes came in that in the first year a T-shaped addition had to be built to the west end of the factory—room for more workers. Soon an L-shaped extension, much larger and accommodating more men and women, was added to the eastern end. The little village of Lestershire, made up chiefly of the homes of the Pioneer workers, grew like a Western boom town. More and more wings were built on to the factory, so many that it began to look like a mass of gigantic blocks hastily thrown together, and every new structure was crowded with workers and machines. In a little more than two years the daily output had increased from an old limit of a thousand pairs to nearly eighteen thousand pairs a day, though the number of workers had not grown in anything like that proportion. But they were the best in the business. Word had spread of the good treatment and high wages in the Pioneer factory, and many ambitious journeymen came from factories in New England and the West.

Henry B. Endicott spent several days in Lestershire in the fall of 1899. He was highly pleased with the growth of the company's business and the evidences of thrift and efficiency he found all through the establishment. Once more he asked George F. Johnson what salary he thought he should have.

"I don't care for a raise," said the superintendent quietly.

Mr. Endicott looked puzzled. What had the man in mind? He did not have to wait long.

"I'd like to buy half the business," said Johnson. "I don't need to tell you, Mr. Endicott, how much better it is now than when I took hold, and I believe that as your partner I can make it still better."

"I believe you can," said Mr. Endicott. "I think we will do well as partners. Do you think $150,000 is a fair price for half the business?"

"Yes, I think it's fair," said George F. "I'll pay that price for it—for all three companies: manufacturing, jobbing and real estate."

"It's yours at $150,000," said Mr. Endicott.

"That is, if you'll take my note for it," Johnson added. "I haven't the money just now, but I'll make it."

"That seems probable," said Mr. Endicott. "Yes; I'll take your note for it."

"Just one detail more," George F. explained. "The note will need $150 in stamps for the war tax. I'll have to borrow that from you."

Mr. Endicott had all the dignity and gravity of a conservative Boston millionaire, but he chuckled at the idea of a man who hadn't one hundred fifty dollars buying half of his business.

"Certainly I'll lend you the money," he said. The note was drawn, payable on demand, at six per cent interest, payable quarterly, and Mr. Endicott bought the stamps for it. As an experienced business man, he knew he was making a good bargain. He could not afford to leave his shoe factory and leather business in Boston in order to run the Pioneer factory, and his new partner had not only rescued the business from bankruptcy but had made it many times as valuable as it had ever been.

Mr. Johnson was a few weeks past his forty-second birthday, vigorous, honest, efficient, a force to be reckoned with in the shoe business, much better to have as a partner than as a rival. His ideas about close friendship with the workers were unorthodox, almost revolutionary, but they produced dividends— in money and in coöperation. If he grew too radical, he could be checked: surely he would be guided by the wisdom of his older partner.

This was a crucial period in the development of

the enterprise. The junior partner had two things to
do—to make the business grow and produce larger
returns, and to make sure that his fellow workers
were treated fairly, even with generosity. Held to a
strict accounting by his senior, who for years had
been his employer, with his settled ideas of the relation between capital and labor, he had a hard struggle
to carry out his theories of team work by the owners
of the business and the men and women who worked
for them—or, rather, who worked with them. A view
of him in the shop at that time was recalled by an
old-timer I found in a treeing room of the original
Pioneer factory.

"I guess George F. had been here a couple of years
when I began to work in the treeing room," he said.
"I was seventeen then. He started me on one dozen
pairs of boots a day, and added more when I could
handle them. He was one of the finest men I ever
worked for. When he wanted a thing done, it had
to be done right or you'd hear from him. He was
easy-going, but you had to be up to the mark."

A faithful outline of Mr. Johnson's understanding
of his relation with his employees appears in an interview published long afterward. His own words tell
better than anyone else can describe the principles
that governed him from the beginning. The inter-
viewer quoted one of the greatest industrialists—
Henry Ford—as writing: "It is not necessary for
the employer to love the employee, or for the em-

ployee to love the employer. What is necessary is for each to try to do justice to the other."

Mr. Johnson flatly contradicted this.

"I don't want to get into a controversy with Mr. Ford," he said, "but if what he wrote is part of his philosophy, then he will die one of the greatest failures the world has ever known.

"I am a shoemaker, without the advantages of education. The conclusions I have reached are purely practical. My theories have grown from my experience in the ranks of workers and executives. My father was a seafaring man, and it was a favorite axiom of his that the best place to learn navigation was at sea.

"I have learned navigation of a different kind— industrial navigation. I was twenty-five when I arrived in Binghamton and went to work for the largest boot manufacturing firm in the city. That was at a time when people say there was the 'fine man-to-man relationship between employer and employee.' I never found that spirit. The owner of the company was a 'big man.' His business was an incident to him. I felt then that something was wrong.

"I don't believe that any man can own a business. It belongs to the customers, to the workers, to the community, to the public. A business cannot be left to incompetent heirs with extravagant ideas of living. You owe to everybody, and to the workers most, to give yourself to it and to arrange as far as possible that the future shall hold the same sort of constructive relationship.

"More coöperation, less friction, more harmony, less discord—that is no mean goal. It is as effective in a working contact between a man and his chauffeur as it is with the head of a large trust and one of his fifty thousand workers. Your chauffeur knows you and your problems, and understands and respects your judgment. Your worker should know you the same way. He can be educated to the difficulties you have in running a vast organization. He can get an understanding of the great problems of capital.

"That doesn't mean coddling. That doesn't mean pampering. That means only that you grant your worker a mind and a heart. You recognize in him the same human qualities that you possess. And—this is most important—to be truly successful, truly constructive, truly great, you must know what is in the mind and in the heart of the worker. Wages alone, no matter how fair, how liberal, won't do it.

"I have no panacea, no formula, for industrial peace. But this I do believe: Those who control labor must live with labor. The children of the workers should grow up with the children of the employers. They should play together. The wives should have a pleasant neighborhood relationship. Executives should be familiar with the lives of their workers—not in a prying sense, but in a social sense. They should be concerned with the happiness and the prosperity of the men and their families. It isn't all-important that the owners shall prosper much, but that people dependent on industry shall prosper in reason.

"A real love for work and workers cannot be manifested at long range. A man can't operate a factory in Binghamton and live in New York. This business of ours is built on the ruins of the one in which I began on my first job. Long-distance supervision shows a short-distance mind. Nothing makes me more impatient, more restless and irritable, than to be controlled by something or someone I can't see and don't know. Why should I hire a manager of a plant who is a stranger to the workers—a man who comes from outside to take a job at the top and talk down to them from a height? I couldn't swallow that; neither can any upstanding individual. It is not hard to make labor happy if you recognize yourself in your men.

"Such a thing as democracy in industry, love in industry, is possible—and it is good business. It's got to be made possible. It's the only answer for human beings. Yet I do not idealize human nature. I know it. I know there is as much aristocracy in labor as there is division between capital and labor. The wife of a chauffeur won't always associate with the wife of a janitor: they're not in the same social class.

"Aristocracy—aristocracy of labor, of wealth—I hate it. Because others are shortsighted is no reason why I should be so. This industry is built on the ideal of democracy, of humanity—and therein lies its strength."

Its strength grew so that the legislature at Albany heard about the success of the business. Senator Frank M. Davenport, a professor in Hamilton College, visited the valley with a committee to find out how labor and capital got on so well together, and George F. Johnson said to him:

"It is a matter of the heart as much as it is of the head. You won't do it unless you have it in your heart, and if you have, you will easily find the way. It is as simple as the Golden Rule. It is putting yourself in the worker's place, and doing by him as you would have him do by you. There is a good deal of talk about the machinery of industrial democracy, but it is the spirit that counts. It is the human factor that makes the machinery worth while.

"We have a rule that any worker or group of workers with a grievance may come at any time of the day directly to me—even in a directors' meeting. We keep up the human touch. One of the greatest sources of unrest among the workers is the thoughtless arrogance of foremen and superintendents, who may think they are 'putting on the screws' for the benefit of the business, but who lose the sense of proportion and fairness. There has to be a court of appeal."

With owners and workers united in one purpose, the new partnership, under the title of the Endicott

Johnson Company, prospered in response to the example and the ceaseless urging of George F. "We should be glad of our success thus far," he often told his workers, "and reasonably contented with the progress we are making—but never satisfied. When a man is satisfied, he's through. We've got to keep trying to do better every day, and we will do better if we keep our minds on it."

Meantime he was rapidly paying off the debt of $150,000 to Mr. Endicott out of his share of the profits of the business, while he and his family continued to live as modestly as when he was only superintendent of the Pioneer factory. As an ambitious young man, conscious of his ability as a business planner and leader, he had looked forward to the time when he would live in a fine house with handsome grounds, drive blooded horses and sail a beautiful yacht. Possibly, if success had come to him early, he would have spent his money on these things. But he was well advanced in middle age before he had money to spend, and by that time he had lost his taste for luxuries. The simple life appealed to him.

Besides, he had witnessed the decay and fall of his former employers, rich shoe manufacturers in New England and Binghamton, who had inherited their prosperity and devoted their energies to sumptuous living rather than to their business. He made up his mind to put his profits into developing his business, and to devote a large share of his income to improving the condition of his fellow workers and of the community in which he lived.

At this time he began to contribute generously to welfare work, churches and hospitals in Binghamton and throughout the valley. His gifts since then have amounted to millions of dollars, always inspired by the idea of helping his neighbors. The striking thing about this giving was—and is—that he felt as much enthusiasm for this object as other men feel for building ornate homes and entertaining on a rich scale. While they went in for collecting costly paintings, rare porcelains, cellars of fine wines, he went in for collecting happy friends. One of the first things he promoted was a fund for paying sick benefits to his people—the E. J. Workers, as they have long been called. This was only the beginning of a series of helpful enterprises which have increased in number and extent year by year.

Soon after Mr. Johnson bought half the business, a rumor was started that he intended to close the Pioneer factory and move away from Lestershire. Reporters from local newspapers asked him whether this was true, and he assured them that he had no such idea. His older brother, C. Fred Johnson, who had followed him to Binghamton as a boss cutter, and from there to the Pioneer, now took charge of the new building operations as the business grew. Presently more land was needed, for with the exception of the Pioneer block and the land given to the

Erie and Lackawanna railroads for stations and yards, Mr. Lester had sold the rest of his one hundred seventy-five acres to his employees and the merchants who flocked to the new village.

Room had to be found now for another factory, for George F. was convinced that the same methods he followed in making coarse working shoes could be applied to making the finer grades. He made a few thousand pairs, and found that they sold readily and at a good profit. He was so sure of success in this new line that he persuaded Mr. Endicott to join him in buying two hundred acres of farms six miles down the river. If he had guessed how greatly the business was to grow in the next few years, Mr. Johnson would have insisted upon buying still more acres, but two hundred seemed enough and to spare for all the company would need for more factories and homes for all their workers. Under the direction of C. Fred Johnson the farms were divided into building blocks, with broad avenues, named for Washington, Lincoln and other presidents, and intersecting streets, along which the E. J. workers could build their homes. The new settlement was called Endicott and incorporated as a village.

It was in the midst of a beautiful country, bounded on the south by the Susquehanna, and framed in long ranges of hills on either side. On the northern border, near the Erie railroad, the company built the Fine Welt factory, for the manufacture of more fashionable shoes—while the heavier grades were still turned out at the old Pioneer shops.

George F. had more in mind than a new factory when he bought the farms at Endicott. After thirty years of striving, he had made it possible to have his dream come true—the big shop flanked by the pleasant homes of the workers. He built an unpretentious home for himself in the midst of the village, not far from the Fine Welt factory, and he planned to have many workers' homes near by. The arrangement would restore the ancient custom in the trades, with the owner's house beside the shop and his journeymen and apprentices living near by, a united family of workers.

To make the dream come true, he saw that the company would have to finance the home building program. Mr. Endicott, cautious, conservative and inclined to shrink from paternalism in business, objected at first; but George F. insisted that helping workers to own comfortable and beautiful homes would promote a spirit of loyalty and good will worth far more than it would cost. Mr. Endicott remembered how well his partner's plans had worked thus far, and at last consented.

In December 1904, the Endicott Johnson Company built seventy-five homes on fifteen acres of land known as Endicott Terrace, on the south side of the village, overlooking the river. Each house cost from $3,000 to $3,500, had six or seven rooms, and stood on a plot of fifty by one hundred feet, which afforded space for a lawn and flowers in the front and a garden in the rear. Each house was individual in design, so that tenants could suit their tastes. The homes in the group were vastly unlike the uniform rows of melancholy "company houses" which still stand in some of the abandoned shoe towns in New England. George F. had lived in them as a boy, and he hated them.

At first the houses rented at fifteen dollars a month; but soon the workers began to buy them with monthly payments of twenty-five dollars while the company charged only three per cent interest on the remainder of the purchase price still due. In every case the worker bought his home for what the land cost by the acre, plus the actual cost of building. Quantity production brought this cost far below what individual builders must pay. The scheme involved a great deal of extra bookkeeping, but George F. saw the happiness it produced and was well content.

Part of the village was thrown open to buyers not in the E. J. organization, and merchants and other outsiders flocked in, among them speculators, who pretended that they were going to build on the land. Prices on these plots rose rapidly as the population grew. A few years later, when the Endicott Johnson Company wanted to build a clinic near the factory for their workers, they had to pay $15,000 for a plot which they had originally sold for $500. Land sharks built tenements at the rear of stores and charged high rents. A worker, his wife and little children were burned to death in a fire in one of these flimsy tenements, and George F. in a letter to the workers expressed his bitter regret at not having provided more land for his people, and promised to avoid such a shortage in the future.

Pioneer Factory at Lestershire. Here George F. started as foreman of the treeing room, and later became superintendent and half-owner with Henry B. Endicott

CHAPTER FIVE

Going into the tanning business—George W. starts as an apprentice—Charles F., Jr. takes his place at the bench—George F.'s vision of an industrial community

IN his constant effort for new ways to turn out better shoes for less money, Mr. Johnson was eager to try tanning. He felt that the increase between the price of raw hides and of the finished leather as it came to the factory was too heavy a load on the shoemakers, and he wanted to throw it off. If his company could save the tanners' profits, they could make shoes much cheaper and divide those profits among the customers, the workers and themselves. Five years had passed between the time when, in 1896, he first proposed to operate a tannery and the time the Endicott Johnson Company built its first tannery at Endicott. From his first objection, "What do you know about tanning leather?" almost up to the day ground

53

was broken for the tannery, Mr. Endicott had been skeptical about the project.

In the first place, shoemakers had always confined their efforts to making and selling shoes, buying their leather from the tanners. The two industries were as far apart as the growing of cotton and the weaving of it. That was the belief of the men who had made shoes for generations—and now this bold innovator challenged it. Mr. Endicott was set in his ways, instinctively opposed to radical changes.

Besides, he had tanneries of his own in Massachusetts, sold their leather to the Endicott Johnson Company at a good profit—in fact, as we have seen, came into shoemaking in his efforts to save the leather he had sold to Harry Lester on credit quite as much as to save money he had advanced. What would become of his principal business if shoemakers everywhere began to tan their own? What would he gain if he ruined it in order to build up his lesser interest? And, if the Endicott Johnson organization failed to make a success of their tanning experiment, that failure might seriously jeopardize their whole enterprise. Any wise man would hesitate as he did.

"It's too big a risk," he told his sanguine partner. "We're doing well enough as it is, and we shall do still better if we let tanning alone."

"We needn't risk too much," said George F. "Let us begin by tanning sole leather only. That is the simplest process in the business. If that works out well, we might try to make the higher grades, the leather for the uppers of our shoes. I know we can do it."

"Well, we might try, I suppose," Mr. Endicott conceded reluctantly. He still had his misgivings, but his partner had already shown such good results and there was something so forceful in the sandy-haired younger man that he could not refuse his consent. They experimented with a small plant at Binghamton, and made a success of it.

That is how the Sole Leather Tannery came to be built, in 1901, at the north side of Endicott, convenient to the Erie railroad, over which raw hides soon arrived in carloads, and left the village as soles and heels of Endicott Johnson shoes. A superintendent, a foreman for each branch of the work, and a crew of first class tanners were brought down from Massachusetts, as soon as the big four-story brick building was completed, with its vats, drums, beams and rollers. A large supply of oak, chestnut and hemlock bark was laid in and bags of bark of the quebracho tree—axe-breaker—from South America; all to be used, with the proper oils, to tan and glaze sole leather. Within a few weeks the crew had settled down to business and was working as briskly as if they had been there for years.

One of the new hands in the tannery crew was a tall, husky, black-haired young fellow named George W. Johnson, whom we have met as president of the Endicott Johnson Company, successor to Mr. Endicott and George F. Johnson in that position. But he was far from any chance of such promotion at that time. Although he was George F.'s eldest son, he went to work as a common laborer. His father made it clear to him as if he were a stranger that it was entirely up to him whether he should rise in the business or be dropped out for not making good.

"No business can carry incompetent workers, George," his father told him. "We can't afford to play favorites. I think you have good stuff in you and you'll do well. Good luck to you."

As his experience is typical of the way in which the executives of the Endicott Johnson Company were brought up from the lowest ranks as they proved themselves fit for promotion, it will pay to look at some of the details. From childhood George W. Johnson was familiar with the shoe business, heard it talked about at home, and played about the Pioneer factory. Today George F. still uses the chair that little George decorated by carving deep grooves in the arms with his first jack-knife. As the boy grew older he earned a little money by running errands about the place in vacation time. The workers knew the quiet lad and liked him; called him George, not Mister George.

By the time he was seventeen young George was in his last year in preparatory school, a good scholar, played on its ball team, and was one of the best southpaw pitchers in the southern tier. Several colleges were ready to welcome him, and he rather liked the idea of going to one of them. When the time came, he found that his father was not for it.

"Too many businesses today, George," he said, "are run by second or third generation men, pleasant fellows who have been through college, think they know a lot, and come into the business from the top. How can they really understand it unless they have begun at the bottom and worked all the way up?" The young man saw the point.

"I saved George from college and put him to work," is the way his father tells it.

The young fellow went in as an apprentice at the bench in the old Pioneer factory. He changed from one department to another, learning the successive stages of putting shoes together. Every day he reported promptly at seven o'clock in the morning with all the rest. By the way, all the executives, from George F. down, still stick to the old-fashioned custom of going to work at seven.

Young George had been a year at the bench when his father offered him the chance to broaden his experience.

"The American Hide and Leather Company," Mr. Johnson said, "have bought out the old Weed tannery at Binghamton and shut it down. We've taken it over, and we're going to see if we can run it. Suppose you go there and learn how to tan leather. That will be a great help to you some day."

So the young man reported at the Weed tannery and was put to work unloading cowhides from freight cars. The hides weighed anywhere from twenty-five to one hundred twenty-five pounds apiece, and there was much more exercise in carrying them out and piling them up, one at a time, than in any baseball game he ever saw. But it agreed with him, and he had the appetite of a hired man, and he put on strength and weight. When the Sole Leather Tannery was opened at Endicott, he went there and began to help stretch hides on poles and lower them into vats. Lifting hides with cranes and moving them about with conveyors did not come in till years afterward, and he spent his days in overalls and high rubber boots, lowering in and lifting out the heavy hides by hand. It was heavy work, among very heavy odors.

From that he went to filling the great revolving drums, steel cylinders in which the hides were sloshed around by steam power while streams of water washed away all the salt and dirt. Then he had some months of removing the hair by passing the hides through a strong lime solution and running them through a de-hairing machine. Then a long spell at the machines that skive off the bits of flesh, and then at the drums in which the lime is washed off the hides.

Next was the "bating," in which they were made ready for the soaking in the tanning vats, to which fresh liquor is added occasionally, to preserve the exact strength required. Thence the hides were loaded into large revolving drums, where oil and other materials were added, to produce firmness and flexibility.

On the top floor of the tannery the apprentice was one of the gang that lifted the hides and hung them high on racks in a hot room, to dry for two weeks. These men work stripped to the waist, and the heavy lifting develops muscles that make them look like wrestlers. Next the hides were sponged with an oil solution and put through heavy "beam" rollers, to pack them down and give the surface an attractive gloss.

From start to finish, the operations of tanning are just one bit of hard labor after another, and the young man who might have been by this time a base ball star at college toiled at them faithfully day after day, and kept at it until he had learned every process thoroughly. When the company began to tan upper- and other light leathers, young Johnson learned all about them, too. He could step up and run any of the machines today—and, incidentally, when any tanner feels dissatisfied with conditions and tells the president about it, he doesn't need an interpreter. Each of them knows all about the situation, for they have had the same experience and speak the same lan-

guage. This practical, first hand knowledge gives the
president a big advantage in everything the company
undertakes in converting hides into finished leather.

One day in 1904 George F. sent for his son, and
the young man reported to him in the Tannery office.

"George," said the father, "the superintendent of
the Tannery is through. Will you go in and take
charge?" That was all. George had not been made
foreman or boss of any kind on the way up, but had
spent five years in overalls, learning all the branches
of the trade. George F. had kept his eye on him, and
knew that he was thoroughly prepared—not only on
the technical side but in the equally important matter
of intimate, friendly relationship with his fellow
workers.

As the company went into the tanning of calfskin,
sheepskin and many kinds of fancy leathers for their
new lines of shoes, George W. managed this work,
as well as the buying of hides in North and South
America, India, Africa, all parts of the world. When
his father became chairman of the board of directors, George W.'s promotion to president was a
natural step, for which he was well prepared.

"Charley has charge of the shoemaking," he says,
"and as long as father is with us, at the head of the
whole business, everyone knows it will go on improving. A great many wonder how it will be with
the next generation. As far as we can see, father has
initiated us into all the details of it, and we're glad

to be on the same terms with our fellow workers as he has always been."

Charley is Charles F. Johnson, Jr., son of George F.'s elder brother, born in Binghamton, in 1887. He is vice president of the Endicott Johnson Company. As a youngster he played with workers' sons, his neighbors and schoolmates, and learned to swim near the Pioneer factory, in the old brickyard pond, where water gathered after the clay had been dug away— now drained, filled, and the site of a beautiful E. J. park. His father did not spoil him with too much money, and he was ambitious to earn for himself. He ran newspapers for a while, and from his thirteenth year he spent most of his vacation time running errands for the shipping department and learning how to pack and ship shoes. The business was as familiar to him as his meals, and he was full of ambition to get a start in it.

Mr. and Mrs. Johnson went down to see Charley graduated from famous old Mercersburg Academy, in his eighteenth year. On the way home Mr. Johnson said, "Now you're ready for college, I'll send you wherever you want to go."

"Thank you, sir," said Charley, "but I believe I don't care to go."

"What? Don't want to go? I thought that's what you were fitting for."

"Yes, sir," said the boy; "but I've been thinking. If I go to college just for the sake of going, I'll be wasting time. I want to learn the shoe business and begin now."

"You're right, boy," said Mr. Johnson. "Glad you've got such good judgment."

On Monday morning the youth went to work in the packing and shipping room of the Boys' and Youths' Factory, near the old Pioneer. He was already well acquainted with the work, and soon he took his place at the bench, learning how to put shoes together. He was so tall and slender that he was not much more than a featherweight, but he kept on growing stronger and bigger for the next six years, until he became a real heavyweight. But in his ambition to learn all about the shoe business he kept no hours, or rather kept all sorts of irregular hours; so that when he was twenty-five he was tired out. He was superintendent of a factory now, but lack of exercise and recreation had worn him down. On his doctor's advice, he went to a health farm, where Bill Brown taught him how to take care of himself and build himself up into the rugged strength he enjoys today.

"That has been of great value to me," he says; "for in this organization we have no soft places. No one here has a good thing that carries him along. He must prove his worth. If he doesn't measure up to his job, he's through, no matter who he is. That's a big help in keeping our business healthy and growing year by year.

F. used to sit there and dream. Stretching to the far western horizon lay the broad valley of the Susquehanna for many a mile, bordered on either hand by ridges of thickly wooded hills. Below the village of Union there were farms that extended from the river to the steep northern slopes.

Here, as the dreamer visioned it, would be plenty of room for whatever new factories he might need, and boundless room for his workers to have their homes and gardens and little farms. No land sharks could rob them of their earnings here; for the land would be reserved for the use of the company and its people.

"They'll all be safe here," he mused. "Lots of room for all of us—yes, and down on that hundred acres by the river I'll build a golf course. If golf's good for the tired business man, it's good for the tired worker, too. Keep it on the level land, too, all the way. Men and women who have been busy at machines all day don't need to climb the tough hills that make a course sporty."

Mornings and afternoons and moonlit nights the chief visited Round Top and planned detail after detail of the project. He took "the boys" up there and enlisted their interest; took other executives of the company, and aroused their enthusiasm. Then he had agents buy the land. He wanted only a thousand acres at first, but the owners would not sell their level land unless the buyers would take their property all the way to the top of the northern ridge; so the purchase grew to thirteen hundred fifty acres.

As we will see, this territory was developed into an ideal region of busy shops and workers' homes, with broad streets, lawns, gardens—all on a scale never before known.

CHAPTER SIX

Branching out into new lines—E. J. Workers'
Page—Comments from the workers

THE rapid increase of the Endicott Johnson factories sprang from two causes—the company's policy of cutting out middlemen's profits and all other unnecessary expenses, and the making of new lines of shoes. We have seen the first important saving, when the company began, in 1899, to buy raw hides and tan sole leather. Two years later they built the big Sole Leather Tannery, at Endicott, bought barks, oils and chemicals in the crude state, and made their own tanning mixtures. In the next year they set up their own laboratories, to test and improve them.

The company advanced, in 1905, to tanning uppers and all sorts of fancy leathers that went into the new varieties of shoes they made. While other manufacturers bought parts of shoes and put them together, Endicott Johnson began, in 1910, to make all their own linings and findings. The crew of each new factory specialized in its particular product and learned to make it economically and at the highest speed. When new machines were invented that did better work, more rapidly, the company used them and scrapped the old ones.

Under this constant stimulus, the business which had begun in a single factory that turned out a few hundred pairs of stogy boots a day for farmers, miners and laborers, grew tremendously as the company branched out into making rough work shoes, then shoes for everyday business wear, in 1901; then many styles of girls' and women's shoes, dress shoes for men and youths, in 1905; followed by shoes for the many kinds of sports, in 1912—for the special needs of Boy Scouts, and for other outdoor requirements.

As this is written (1934) the company operates twenty-nine plants, which manufacture every kind of shoe worn by Americans of all ages, as well as the materials of which they are made. They seize every chance to save. In the Fibreboard Mill at Johnson City, they have made, since 1917, the light but strong stuff used to shape and build counters. In another mill they weave their own linen fabrics for shoe linings. In another they make the thousands of stout, tough cartons of *papier mâché* and the cardboard boxes in which each pair of shoes is packed.

Every change of fashion is watched, and new models are made to meet it. Usually the change is anticipated; for the designers study the trends in styles

Beam-house, E.J. Tannery at Endicott

and prepare to meet the demand that will come next. To do this accurately insures the production of goods that sell quickly, with a constant call for more, while failure to catch the popular fancy would fill the warehouses with shoes that must be sold slowly and at a loss.

One of the most striking examples of the expansion of the Endicott Johnson industry is its entry into the business of rubber manufacture, at Johnson City. Near the old Pioneer Factory and its many busy additions stands the great Paracord Factory and its branch, the Jigger Factory, in which all kinds of rubber boots and shoes that people wear are turned out in an endless stream. Near by are the yards in which old automobile tires are stacked by the acre, higher than a man's head, and in the warehouses are tons of pure crude Para rubber.

For two years the Endicott Johnson Corporation had been buying rubber heels to put on certain popular types of shoes, as well as rubber soles for heavy work shoes. If these modes were mere fads, the demand would soon cease, and nothing need be done about it. But the demand grew, the company was buying more rubber soles and heels every year; so they studied how to make their own, thus cutting out unnecessary costs. That would enable them to make and sell better shoes cheaper than others, who bought these parts ready made, and merely assembled them.

So, in 1922, Endicott Johnson built their own rubber reclaiming and manufacturing plant, at a cost of $500,000, and began to make their own rubber, from the raw to the finished product. This meant the engagement of new experts to manage the job and skilled workers to do it; for it was a more radical departure from the old ways of making shoes than going into tanning had been. And, as in the first experiment, Mr. Johnson was justified in his belief that money would hire men who knew how to make and handle rubber with a profit. They turn waste to good use.

An automobile tire from the junk pile is set into a machine that whirls it around and skives off the beads. Then it is fed into an apparatus that chops it into chunks, and from there into a "rubber hog"—a cylinder full of knives which slice it into shreds. This mass is put into a great, double-jacketed steel kettle, mixed with caustic soda and a softener like pine tar oil, and kept at a temperature of 360° Fahrenheit for eight hours. This reduces the cotton fabric interwoven with the rubber into fluid cellulose, but makes no change in the rubber itself except to devulcanize it and resolve it into liquid form.

The rubber is drawn off into kettles, in which it is washed, to free it from the caustic soda. Then it is dried and refined; that is, passed between two massive, shiny steel rolls, close together, one revolving faster than the other, and comes out in sheets, ready to use. These rolls exert such tremendous pressure that, if a man were drawn into them, he would come out as thin as a postal card. But as the worker feeds the slabby mass into the rolls, there is a safety lever close to his hand. It extends all the way along the machine, within easy reach, so that at the least sign of danger the operator can snatch it down and stop the rolls instantly.

Twenty-four tons of old tires are put through this mill every working day, and out of them the experts get twelve tons of rubber. This reclaimed material, mixed with the proper proportion of crude, makes ideal soles for work shoes, soles that wear better than those of pure rubber. They give three times as much service as leather soles, and cost one-third as much. Every step in the process is watched, with a view to saving time and material, thus reducing costs. Here is one instance:

In preparing rubber for making box toes, it was found that a large amount of acetone set free by the process went up the chimney in fumes that were wasted on the idle air—twenty-five thousand dollars' worth of them every year. Could this valuable stuff be saved? The E. J. rubber management found that a scientist had invented a machine to gather the fumes, one hundred per cent, and turn them into liquid acetone, easily collected and stored. They bought the machine for $35,000. It paid for itself in little more than a year, and it has saved $25,000 a year since.

The company has taken care, in placing the factories, to group those doing similar work close together, thus saving time and transportation costs in handling material and products. The great majority of the factories have been built at Johnson City, Endicott and West Endicott, with ample space between for homes, parks and markets. The Sunrise and Jigger factories, next door to the big Paracord at Johnson City, illustrate the value of the grouping idea. They use most of the rubber produced at the mother plant. In Sunrise four hundred men and women make rubber sandals, overshoes, gaiters, boots and pacs— every kind of waterproof to keep the wet from the feet in rain or snow. They turn out six hundred dozen pairs of these every day during the summer, for use in the next winter. When winter comes, these workers go over to the Jigger Factory and make tennis and sport shoes, to be ready for the next summer. These are partly cloth, while the Sunrise stuff is all rubber except the linings; but the processes are very similar in both shops, and the workers change from one to the other without any loss in time or wages.

Frank Johnson, son of George W. and grandson of George F., showed me through Sunrise. He began at the bench in Jigger right after graduation from high school, in 1930, worked in all the departments of both shops, and learned the business so well that now he is assistant superintendent. He is tall, rather dark, keenly watchful of all that goes on, but never too busy to talk about shoemaking with his companions, many of them his playmates a while ago. At lunchtime, when I first saw him, he was in a long line, chatting with his fellow workers, all slowly approaching the counter of the company restaurant. In the factory he seemed to know all about every process, had an answer ready for every question.

Swiftly the masses of dull gray, sticky gum and bolts of linings were changed into rows of shining, weatherproof shoes. The raw stuff, colored in the kettles to the right hues of black, white, brown or gray that the order required, was fed into the calender, whence it was passed up through four smooth steel rolls, which reduced it to uniform thickness and stamped designs on it—the name of the maker, style and number of its size when finished. The gleaming cylinders were not unlike the rolls of a giant printing press, and the sheet of rubber flowed past like newspapers in the making.

The endless sheet of rubber, still warm and plastic, was hauled unbroken up to the next floor, reeled in and put through a new set of rolls, in which the lining fabrics were pressed on to it with lasting firmness: net for sandals, or fleece for women's boots and gaiters. The linings were cut by hand, and bright knives were flying around the metal patterns. The upper parts, in "books" of a dozen, were conveyed to the casing room on the floor above, where they were put in long boxes with their lasts; boots in one dozen lots; smaller shoes in lots of two to four dozen.

On the floor above they were lasted and the reinforcement put in, a rubber-coated friction stuff called *osenberg* for the heavies, or *sheeting* in lighter shoes. Thence to the machines, where they were "spotted;" that is, the soles and heels were fastened on by hydraulic pressure of thirty-five pounds to the square inch. Next the gussets, fasteners and other parts were put in place, and the edges of the shoes were rolled. There are from twelve to eighteen pieces in every shoe, all joined by machinery, which moves with speed that dazzles the visitor but seems easy as breathing to the workers.

There was something hypnotic in the unbroken rhythm of men and machines, in the steady throb and hum of power, and the keen concentration of every worker on the job. Yet none of it seemed tiresome, and once in a while the busiest of them had time for a few words with a neighbor.

Now the polish came on: the gaiters sprayed with transparent lacquer, the sandals dipped, a dozen at a time in varnish, automatically raised on racks, toes down and a black drop rolling, about to fall off; then the machines reversed their position and the drops ran down the sides of the shoes and disappeared as they spread. Boots and heavy pacs were varnished with the spray; high pacs powdered with corn starch to keep the color uniform.

As they dried, the shoes were loaded on to cars of

slender framework, each carrying six dozen pairs of gaiters or twelve dozen pairs of sandals, trundled to the elevator and carried down to the second floor, to be "cured." This is a job that calls for precision, as nice judgment as a pilot uses in steering among shoals, or rather the delicate wisdom of a housewife cooking the Thanksgiving turkey to just the right shade of brown. With this difference: if the turkey is a bit overdone, no one cares much; but if the rubbers cook one minute too long or too little, three hundred dollars' worth of stuff is ruined.

In an orderly row on the second floor a battery of vulcanizers wait for business. Each vulcanizer is a steel cylinder, seven feet in diameter, lying on its side. Men roll into the vulcanizer three of the tall, slender cars, each loaded with rows of nice, shiny new rubbers. They step back, and the expert swings to and fastens with powerful steel levers a massive steel door that fits tighter than the door of a bank vault. Strong as a dynamite-proof door, and with good reason, too; for now the operator fills the vulcanizer with an air pressure of thirty pounds to the square inch. This pressure holds the coating of rubber in its exact position and thickness on each shoe, as if the tips of millions of tiny, invisible fingers were supporting the thin film.

This is needed because the vulcanizer is flooded with steam, which in half an hour raises the temperature to 252° Fahrenheit. Without the even pressure of the air, the patterns would sag and spoil, and the rubber would melt and run like hot butter; and to keep the pressure perfectly uniform fans whirl the air in steady circulation. Result, not one particle of rubber moves so much as the breadth of an eyelash, and at the end of two hours or so the door is unlocked and swung open, and the cars of rubbers are run out to cool. The heat, plus the sulphur and other chemicals mingled in the original mass, makes a perfect "cure."

"What would happen if a vulcanizer made a mistake?" I asked Frank Johnson.

"They don't," he replied.

As the growth of the business brought in more workers and caused the building of new factories, Mr. Johnson gave them names likely to arouse the workers' enthusiasm. The Pioneer was roomy, well lighted and ventilated, and its name emphasized the departure from the old policy at Lestershire. Each new building thereafter was an improvement over its predecessors. Fine Welt at Endicott, built in 1901, marked the beginning of making finer shoes. The name of Ideal Factory, built in 1903, was a stimulus to better work, a reminder of E. J. ideals. Victory Factory at Johnson City, opened soon after the close of the World War, honored not only the triumph of the Allied cause but service of E. J. workers. Paracord, in operation at Johnson City since 1922, signifies the union of Para rubber with fabrics spun and woven. Sunrise, its neighbor, suggests the fresh vigor of a new day. When a new shop was constructed at Johnson City to accommodate the increase of E. J. business in the dark days of 1931, George F. called it the Challenge Factory.

With so many newcomers in the factories, Mr. Johnson found it impossible to keep in touch with them through the *E. J. Workers' Review,* which he had founded in April, 1919. Once a month was not often enough to discuss the problems of the fast growing business; so he gave up the *Review* in the fall of 1925, and bought a full page every day in the Binghamton *Sun,* for which he paid advertising rates. This supplemented the letters and bulletins he put up occasionally on the time clock which every employee punches. He still uses it.

The E. J. Workers' Page has been read ever since the first issue with keen interest. Here are recorded George F.'s letters to his people, besides the daily happenings in the E. J. communities and the news of the E. J. shops, markets, schools, churches, sports and recreations. This open forum is not so intimate as the frequent talks with his men in the old days, but it serves to keep everybody well informed. When any worker has a complaint, George F. urges him to write to the Page and ask satisfaction. Even anonymous complaints are investigated. Every grievance is thoroughly looked into, and the results are published on the Page. This brings out the facts and keeps the air clear of smouldering dissatisfaction. As more workers have been needed from time to time, E. J. employees have sent specimen pages to their friends in other cities.

"I didn't take much stock in this business when I first read of it," said a husky laster beside whom I sat at a clambake on the farm of one of the workers, not far from the factory in which he was employed. "I had worked a long time in factories in Missouri and the West, and had to lay off every now and then; so at last I came here, in 1933. Say! it's like moving into a different country. It ain't only that we earn more money and the shops are better to work in but we have a chance to live in real homes, not jammed into rows of sloppy old houses.

"And all the good things thrown in on the side! I never saw anything like this layout. I don't see how these Johnsons do it—but they've been keeping it up a long time, and they don't seem to lose by it. Look over there now: all four of them scattered among the bunch, having as much fun as any of us. No high hats, no stuffed shirts; just regular fellows. The best of it is, they give everyone an even break. I wish I'd come here twenty years ago. I'm fifty now, but it ain't too late at that. I've made a good start at buying a home, and in a few years more it'll be all mine. And I'll tell you one thing—in this place you feel that you are somebody, not a dumb factory hand, to be hired and fired and kicked around. It's living; that's what it is."

A woman worker told of her experience.

"When I came here, in 1919," she said, "I found everything so different from my home town that I simply couldn't understand how these people could do business in such an easy-going way. I had worked for years as a shoe stitcher and packer in three shops in New England, and I had friends in Revere, Haverhill, Brockton and other places. And wherever I worked they had a forewoman for every ten or a dozen workers, to see that they kept steadily at it; no time for talking or anything else. It was drive, drive, drive, every minute. Here in Endicott, everybody seemed to take things easy—and yet kept busy all the time. We were all on piece work, you see, and if we took a few moments now and then we made up for it.

"Nobody drives you here, and yet, if you fall behind in production, a director—they don't call them forewomen or foremen—gives you a friendly call. What's holding you back? Do you find your job unpleasant? Would you rather try something else? No? Well, then don't you think you can do better—for your own sake and everybody's? No nagging; just a bit of friendly advice. These people don't drive you to do better: they treat you so you want to do your best. And so you try to improve—and you do. Believe me, I've tried, and I know. It isn't hard to pay a little closer attention when you know it will get you a

bigger pay envelope at the end of the week. No forewomen anywhere to jump at you. In my stitching
room we have only one director and her two assistants
for two hundred sixty-four girls at the machines.

"In New England the factories are in an old settled country, in towns where they crowd against one
another; no room to spread out and work and live, the
way we do here. Up there the owners haven't learned
how to deal with their workers in a friendly way—
maybe they've never thought about trying it.

"Not that there's anything sloppy about these E. J.
people. They trust everybody, but they keep their
eyes open. As long as you do your work right, you'd
almost have to do murder to get fired. I know of cases
where fellows have been caught stealing leather.
What happened? The boss sent for them, told them
he knew what they'd done, and said: 'Go on back to
work, and quit making a fool of yourself.' And the
funny thing is, the fellows kept straight after that; so
I guess it was better than firing them after all.

"Everybody's on piece work. If you want to get up
from your machine and stretch your muscles or chat
with a friend for a few minutes, no one drives you
back, as they do where I came from. Still we turn
out a great deal more work than they do up there.
I'm glad I left that country, where business is falling
off, companies cutting each other's throats, having
labor troubles and strikes, and poor relief for people

who ought to be at work if the owners only knew how to run their business.

"Unless you've lived and worked in other places, you can't understand what a difference there is. A shoemaker from home and his wife, a stitcher, both old friends of mine, stopped over here a few days on their way back from the West, and I showed them around. They could hardly believe what they saw—the big workrooms so well lighted and well aired, the easy way everybody worked, the medical care, and the fine schools, libraries and playgrounds. They had never dreamed of anything like it.

"In the bus on the way to the train they said: 'When you wrote home about what was going on here and the way they do things, we thought—well, to tell you the plain truth, we thought you were lying: no business could be run that way. But now we've seen it. Wonder if we'll think it's all a dream after we get back?' "

In sharp contrast with their amazement is the attitude of the workers who have lived for years in the valley, especially those who were born there and have never known any other way of living. They take their easy circumstances for granted, as simply and naturally as the children of the rich take the luxury that surrounds them. Once in a while a worker visits friends in communities not so fortunate, and when he comes back tells the neighbors what he has seen; but the general feeling is that life in the Endicott

Johnson region is so well organized that it will go on indefinitely without change.

When business slackens everywhere, and the E. J. workers are employed only three or four days a week —as has happened occasionally in the depression years—they simply cut down on luxuries, and go fishing, golfing or gardening. They do not feel alarmed; for the industrial ship has weathered other storms and she'll weather this one, too.

"How many of your people really understand conditions here as compared with those in other industries?" I asked George F.

"Nine-tenths of them," he replied. "And they keep the other one-tenth in line."

While there are playgrounds in all the E. J. communities and parks of natural beauty aided by constant cultivation, a visitor to the factories is surprised to find each one set in the midst of acres of bare concrete pavement. This is so different from the elaborately landscaped grounds of showy manufacturing plants in other regions that it rouses curiosity.

"Doesn't the company ever think of having gardens and fountains around its buildings?" I asked a tanner.

"Gardens and fountains!" he exclaimed. "Hell! We haven't room enough for our cars. You know we all have cars, and C. Fred and his gang are busy all the time fixing up more parking space, so we won't have to walk so far to the shops."

Which is the truth. Every afternoon soon after four o'clock, when the men and women pour out of the factories at the end of their day's work, you will see thousands of automobiles crawling through traffic jams. During all the months I lived there I could not get used to the phenomenon of so many workers in cars—especially as I recalled the weary men and women I have seen in other manufacturing towns at quitting time, silently plodding along in droves, dinner pails and lunch baskets in hand, their faces gloomy or blank. The E. J. workers, even the gray-haired ones, bounce out like a lot of youngsters leaving high school, smiling and talking as they go.

CHAPTER SEVEN

*Housing For the Workers—Realization of
George F.'s Dream at West Endicott—
A Golf Course For the Workers*

AFTER the Endicott Johnson Corporation was
organized, in 1919, George F. Johnson was able to
carry out his plans for building homes for the workers. From 1899 until then he had drawn out of the
profits only enough for his modest living, and Mr.
Endicott, with a large income from his Massachusetts enterprises, joined him in using the earnings to
build more factories and raise wages. Five other
officers owned lesser interests.

The conservatism of the majority of his fellow
officers kept them from seeing that George F.'s plan
to improve living conditions would bring greater
success. The attitude of most industrialists on the
question is reflected in reports of the United States
Bureau of Labor, which show that as late as 1920
practically all housing by employers consisted of

84

Boys and Youths Factory, just after completion, before C.F.J. Park was created

Boys and Youths Factory, Johnson City. A part of C.F.J. Park in foreground

renting company houses to their workers. Most of these were in the iron, steel and coal industries and among textile manufacturers in New England and the South. A few had built schools and libraries in workers' villages, but the reports do not indicate any such far-sighted plan as Mr. Johnson had in mind.

These government reports show a sharp contrast between the humane and friendly spirit in which George F. helped his workers to build their houses around his own, and the policy of most other employers, who set workers' villages off by themselves and kept close control of the houses by renting them. Sociologists today deplore segregation as likely to cause strife.

Instead of spending money on workers' homes, the reports show, most employers made a profit on them —five per cent in some cases, a "modest return" in others. One New England textile manufacturer excused the bad condition of his company houses by saying that his employees were a poor, untidy lot. The owners of a hemp and jute mill closed the smoking room of the company library because the men were disorderly, and did not reopen it for seventeen years. In nearly every case there appeared a cleavage between employers and workers, a lack of the friendly coöperation and neighborliness that inspired George F.'s relation with his people.

About a year after the incorporation of the company, Mr. Endicott died and Mr. Johnson succeeded him as president of the company. For the first time in his life George F. Johnson realized that he was rich. By the change from partnership to the corporate form his ownership in the business was represented by ten million dollars' worth of stock. He had often talked over with "the boys"—his son and nephew, entirely in sympathy with the idea—his plans for housing and medical care for the workers. Now he had the money to spend on them. To supply this, as well as his contributions to hospitals, to Broome County relief and his gifts of three houses and $150,000 of Endicott Johnson stock to local American Legion posts and $50,000 for the War Memorial, he drew on his principal as well as the income. The latter contributions he made while he was still looking for the best way to solve the workers' housing problem.

This problem grew out of the increase of the company's business, the added number of workers and the influx of several smaller manufacturing concerns, as well as of storekeepers and others who set up business in the communities. The population of Lestershire grew from five thousand to nearly ten thousand between 1904 and 1912, when the citizens voted to change its name to Johnson City. Endicott, which was open country in 1900, had a population of eight thousand, still increasing, in 1919.

Every new line of shoes added to the fast growing business called for the building of a new factory.

The Chrome Tannery at Endicott (1908) was followed by the Scout Factory at Johnson City (1912) and the Heeling Factory and Box Toe Department in the next two years. A large wing was added to the Sales Building at Endicott in 1914, and in a few years the large Upper Leather Beam House and Hide Building were erected near by. Between 1916 and 1921 there followed the Fire Prevention Building in each village, the Mechanical, the New Scout, Pioneer Annex, Fibreboard Mill, the Service Department and the Heeling and Trimming factories. Every one of these brought from five to eight hundred new workers and their families into the community. Rents rose steadily, as the demand for housing increased faster than the supply.

Harry L. Johnson, George F.'s youngest brother, did what he could to relieve the crowding at Johnson City. The only one of the four brothers who had not learned the shoemaking trade, he left Plymouth, where he was assistant postmaster, in 1902, to join the office force at the Pioneer factory. He quickly earned the friendship of the workers as he learned the business, and in a few years he became superintendent of all the Johnson City factories. When the demands for war supplies had created a boom in every business, Johnson City was more crowded than ever, and landlords raised rents so high that many Endicott Johnson workers were hard pressed to find living room.

Harry Johnson bought a large tract north of the village, in 1916, and on it built eighty houses, which he intended to sell to the workers at cost. But so much grading and filling had to be done that the costs were greatly increased. Rather than raise the prices he had named in advance, he took a loss of a thousand dollars on each house. C. Fred Johnson built eighty-five homes for workers on the Goodwill Tract, north of Johnson City, at the same time.

"Harry Johnson," George F. said to the workers after his brother's death, in 1922, "was the best friend you have ever known. I have waited until I could speak of Harry without breaking, when I could calmly say a word to you. Just as surely as any soldier gave his life for his country, so surely did Harry Johnson give his. It was the war and what grew out of the war that preyed on his mind and hastened his death.

"When I came back from the South last April, things looked pretty blue. Harry had been writing and wiring me. Competitors were getting our business. It never occurred to him that we could ask our working partners to accept a wage cut. He had put the best part of his life into helping to build up these wages and all the other good things.

"When I said to him, 'Harry, there is nothing that can be done but this one thing,' it seemed to him impossible. His love for those with whom he toiled was past understanding. The very thought that he might hurt them was terrible to him. Harry Johnson loved the working people, of whom he thought himself one. When he went away, I knew his heart was broken. He never came back."

The workers erected a monument to Harry L. Johnson, surmounted with a bronze statue of him, in C. F. J. Park, Johnson City.

With ten thousand men and women at work in the various E. J. shops, in 1916, the company organized its own fire prevention service. C. Fred Johnson, who managed the building department, took charge of this, and he developed it on a scale and with a thoroughness rarely seen outside of a metropolitan fire department. A large fire house was built in the centre of each community, equipped with the most efficient apparatus, with companies of trained men on duty night and day. Every scrap of waste was swept away from the machines and carried out. Fine shreds were drawn off by air suction into containers. Tests of the apparatus and fire drills by the workers were often made. One day when a drill was suddenly called in the Endicott Fine Welt Factory a well dressed gentleman on the third floor didn't want to take his chances with the crowd.

"I'm a traveling salesman," he protested. "I'm not one of the workers—"

"Hell! You'd burn quick as any of 'em," C. Fred shut him off. "You hop out on that fire escape."

Mr. Johnson looked west of Endicott for more room, which would soon be needed for the growing business. At his suggestion the company bought, late in 1919, thirteen hundred fifty acres only two miles down river from Endicott. It lay just beyond the ancient village of Union, which recently had been merged with Endicott. West Endicott was the name he chose for the new community, in which his dream of factories surrounded by pleasant homes of workers was at last to be realized.

While the surveyors and engineers were engaged in plotting factory sections and dwelling areas near by, expert drillers were driving deep artesian wells to provide a plentiful supply of pure water. The ground was gently rolling, and there was plenty of room for parks, playgrounds and wading pools for the littlest children. Two tanneries and two welt factories were to be built.

Before the factories and homes were half done, gangs of men were grading and surfacing new roads to the summit of Round Top, where fifteen acres were laid out as a park and picnic ground. The view from here over miles of country, its green fields and tracts of forest alternating with masses of factories surrounded by villages of attractive homes and gardens, is one of the finest in the State. By night, when the clusters of village lights illuminate the plain, and motor cars skim along the highway by the river, it is a bit of fairyland. And when George F. looks out over this panorama of industry and human welfare that he has created, it is probable that he derives as much pleasure from it as some captains of industry find in their collections of rare paintings.

In the usual real estate development the promoters buy many acres of open country, put in streets, sewers, water, gas, electricity and divide the land into building sites, which they sell to the customers at a handsome profit. The Endicott Johnson plan is different. In West Endicott, for example, they made all the improvements—and in selling homes to the workers charged them less than what it all cost. They plowed the land, fertilized and harrowed it, and started the lawns and gardens as soon as the houses were finished. Each home plot was fifty by one hundred fifty feet, with ample room for a garage.

No two houses were quite alike. While there was a good deal of diversity of styles among them, they all blended with one another in a harmonious composition. The streets and sidewalks were broad and well paved, and thousands of quick-growing trees were planted along the curbs and on the lawns, with hedges of privet or Japanese shrubs. The company took care of sewers, streets and lights. The houses had six or seven rooms, with every modern convenience, and sold at from $2,500 to $3,500 each. One cost $4,200. Building them in large numbers reduced expense for planning, labor, materials and supervision. But even at that the company took a loss of $100,000 on the first hundred houses. Workers paid a few hundred dollars down and arranged to add six dollars a week out of their wages until the whole price was paid. In case of sickness or other distress, payments could be suspended.

Some of the workers thought they would like larger houses, with more ornamentation. When they spoke to George F. about this, he discouraged the idea.

"These homes," he said, "are comfortable and beautiful. They are fine enough for any family in the land. Don't waste your money on fancy stuff and frills. The great trouble with all of us—I am the chief offender—is that we want too much. Whether we can afford it or not, we feel bound to have it. It's pretty bad to have too much, even when we can afford it, but it's a great deal worse to have too much when we can't afford it, because the pleasure is lost in the anxiety and worry of being in debt. When you have a surplus, invest it wisely, and you'll be glad of it some day when you need it.

"Use your common sense and good judgment. Get the house paid for as quickly as you can, so you'll have a home, no matter what happens. Then buy the automobile if you must—and buy it for cash. Paying cash is a valuable habit. Try it."

The company charged interest on the unpaid remainder of purchase price at five per cent a year—which was reduced, in 1930, to three per cent. At the time of this writing—1934—Endicott Johnson workers owe the company $1,200,000 on their homes. In paying only three per cent instead of six they save $36,000 a year. There is no municipal or corporation tax in West Endicott.

In the midst of the village the company erected a large brick building of modern style, at a cost of $100,000, and gave it to the people. The fire prevention company occupies the ground floor. The upper stories are used as a community centre, with bowling alleys, billiard tables, dining rooms and recreation hall. As you walk through the neighborhood you are impressed by the care and good taste the citizens devote to keeping their village in condition. There are many children. (George F. says a man is not a man until he has a home, wife and children.) This community of five thousand people has been in existence since 1922 and it has never had any police force. I asked Mr. Johnson how they manage to get along without police and he looked surprised.

"Why, they're all E. J. workers," he said.

Visitors who came miles to see West Endicott admired its beauty but seldom guessed the endless effort that produced and preserved it. The company leveled and fitted out smooth baseball diamonds, for workers and youngsters, protected playgrounds with high fences of wire mesh that let parents see in and kept adventurous children from climbing out among traffic, while wading pools, see-saws and swings gave

them plenty of fun within bounds. It was easy to
know what they wanted—George F. remembered
what he lacked as a child, and furnished it for them.
The finest building in the village is the George F.
Johnson public school, a handsome big brick structure with white trim and large classrooms, well
lighted and ventilated. It cost $300,000, and it is
called the most modern and most completely
equipped school among the counties in the Southern
Tier.

But the most interesting part of West Endicott is
the most modest section. Here are twenty-four little
bungalows, the smallest homes in the village. They
satisfied a desperate need; they saved workers' families from blighting exposure to cold—and they have
proved so useful that they are still occupied and
probably will stay in service for years to come.

Here is their origin: The need of homes for
workers during and right after the World War was
acute. Landlords of the type George F. calls "land
sharks" were raising rents everywhere; families paying thirty or thirty-five dollars a month were turned
out to make room for others at fifty dollars or higher
—turned out in the street, with no place to store their
furniture. Something had to be done at once to provide shelter for the helpless ones. War veterans suggested that the company might buy tents cheaply and
set them up on the land rent free.

"That would never do," said Mr. Johnson. "Comfortable four months in the year and freeze to death the other eight. We must find houses, weatherproof and warm. Let's take a lot of the garages we've been building in quantities for our workers, cut out the ends and put them back to back on the last street we've laid out at West Endicott. Each pair of garages will make a nice, three-room bungalow. Good sized rooms." In a few days the bungalows were ready. The houses were set up, twelve on each side of the newly surfaced avenue, and connected with sewer, water, gas and electricity. At the back of each bungalow was a large woodshed, with room to store washtubs and a toilet in the corner. The company charged only five dollars a month rent for each house, though they collected four times that much.

"You've been paying from twenty-five to fifty dollars a month rent and getting mighty little for it," George F. told his workers. "We'll let you have a house for twenty a month, which is five dollars a month rent and fifteen a month put to your credit, on which we'll pay you six per cent interest. At the end of the year we'll sell you the little home, say at $2,000, and the yearly total produced by your fifteen dollars a month, with interest, will be your first payment."

The refugees took the bungalows instantly, found them snug, big enough and comfortable. Best of all, they were building up a home-buying fund by paying only half as much as they had paid for tenements.

The first owners in a few years saved enough to pay for their bungalows, sell them back to the company and buy bigger houses. But other workers in the constantly increasing army were waiting to move in, and the cottages were never empty. Each house has its grass plot and flowers; the sidewalks are shaded and the whole row has a festal air. Yet the bungalows have been for scores of families the first step toward owning a handsome home.

"It is a curious thing," said Mr. Johnson to me, "that we, by force of necessity, evolved probably the best plan yet contemplated and made effective to help a poor man secure a home and make his first payment on it with money saved during the year. I recommend it as a practical idea: How to start a poor man on the right road in the direction of owning his home —furnishing him with a comfortable, temporary home. This plan can be worked anywhere, and will provide homes for people who never on earth would have them, because they could not get a start."

The nearest approach to the Endicott Johnson plan of housing for workers has been under way in England since 1933. Henry J. Allen, former United States senator and governor of Kansas, published in January, 1935, his survey of the building, within the preceding nineteen months, of four hundred twenty thousand small homes in Great Britain. Private enterprise, with municipal aid, furnished the capital, and workers bought homes on instalments, at $3,000 and upward. France, Germany and other governments have begun to build good, cheap homes, aware that the state is in peril when half the people live in slums while the other half is well housed—peril as great as threatened our country half slave and half free in Lincoln's day.

Though this British housing program recognizes that decent living for workers is a prime social need, which private capital must satisfy, it is far different from the George F. Johnson plan. The essence of his idea is that employers and employed shall live close to one another, friends and neighbors, a community of families with mutual interests. The British plan keeps employers and employed in separate districts. That is in accord with the ancient English class system, derived from the feudal principle, which divides mankind into lords and vassals, masters and servants.

The cheerful homes for Endicott Johnson workers, so different from industrial housing and welfare promotions, grew out of the neighborly instinct of one man.

"I had always been anxious to have money," George F. Johnson wrote, in 1920, "but as I began to get more and more of it, I began to wonder if it would not be better to give more attention to the human side. Out of that grew our present plan of organization."

It was not entirely what happened inside the factory, he believed, so much as what happened outside that affected working conditions. "Comparing our results with the constant ferment of the Massachusetts shoe towns," he continued, "I became thoroughly impressed with what I now consider the fundamental point in the labor relation—environment. I believe that the best and most economical work is to be had from the large unit, and that this unit can be made a community unto itself. . . ." *

Since golf is an important part of the development of West Endicott, this is the place to tell of it. The joys of golf are a great asset in the Endicott Johnson industry. Every executive plays but George F. He has time for it only on vacation. Shoemakers, from boys and girls just out of high school to grayhaired men and women, flock to the game every fair day. Apawamis, Baltusrol, Cochecho, Deal, Englewood and hundreds of other links are fine tests of skill, many of them championship courses. But not one of them is adapted to its purpose quite so well as the En-Joie Health Golf Club course that Mr. Johnson established for his workers at West Endicott.

Children's playgrounds come first in his program, but golf for his friends who help him make shoes runs a close second. You feel it the moment you stand on the first tee and look out over the ground. The whole layout is carefully calculated to yield the

* *System Magazine (January, 1920).*

greatest pleasure to the greatest number. Most important in the scheme is the broad field, level or nearly so. In the generous thirteen hundred fifty acres of the West Endicott tract there was plenty of room to make a sporty course, up and down high hillsides, that would test players' legs and hearts. But men and women who have been busy at the bench all day, keeping up production at the swift pace that prevails in the E. J. factories, do not need sporty holes on hilltops.

What they need is the greatest amount of play possible, with mild exercise and the utmost of recreation on the green grass, with a varied and charming landscape to relieve their minds of the strain of an occasional topped stroke. This they have at En-Joie—and when you have done your eighteen holes you will not complain of lack of work. The magic of it is that it all feels so easy while playing that no one notices the work.

No championship course has better fairways than En-Joie; the grass is well cut, the turf so deep and soft that brassie and spoon get well down under the ball all the way round. Since most of the players are in the one hundred class the fairways are wide enough to hold almost any slice or pull the wildest player can contrive. And if his ball freakishly sails off into the rough, the player is not punished like a criminal, as happens on so many courses. The rough is rough, all right, but the grass in it is kept so short that the slicer or hooker can find his ball as he walks up. He will be punished by having to play out of a rough lie, but his fault won't be made a hanging matter—as too often is the case on otherwise civilized links.

The player on En-Joie is free of all these blemishes on a perfect day. Moreover, hunting lost balls is the greatest waster of time on a golf course, and the time saved here is so much that an average player can go comfortably over the whole six thousand one hundred fifty yards in little more than two hours and a half. This is important to the man or woman who does not leave the factory till four o'clock, even with daylight saving time.

And golf balls cost money. One of the saddest sights on any course is the shillyshallying of some poor fellow torn between his desire to avoid delay and his dislike of losing a seventy-five-cent ball. At En-Joie this cannot happen; and, as a result, the player's enjoyment of the game is keener.

The fame of the course has spread so far that visitors come from Ithaca, Rome and Elmira, as well as from Scranton and other Pennsylvania cities. So long as they behave like true golfers, they are as welcome on the links as the E. J. workers, and at the same rate of green fees. Under the ruling idea—the greatest good for the greatest number. Some of the adepts are a little patronizing before they tee off; it looks so easy as they survey the long, level prospect. I played with one of these on a fine day, a good man who had

En-joie Health Golf Course. Clubhouse in right background; a few workers' homes in foreground

shot pars where pars are hard to get. He expected to shoot the course in seventy-five, but after a few mishaps he was glad to get an eighty-three. I told him some of the young shoemakers score sixty-eights and sixty-nines.

"Must be something about their business that makes them shoot good golf," he said. 'You remember the old legend of the Royal and Ancient Company of Golfers, that King James of Scotland was trimmed on the links by ane, Paterson, a shoemaker.'"

"I know our golf is a great aid to health and happiness," George F. says. "It's a mistake to think of it as a rich man's game. It should be every man's game, and we aim to keep it so at En-Joie."

It is difficult to write the last word about West Endicott. If you happen to stroll through the streets of the village any morning at half-past eight or so, you will see Mr. Johnson driving along the avenues or some of the cross streets. As soon as he has finished answering the letters in his home office, where he begins work at seven, he gets behind the wheel of his dark green roadster, and drives down Main Street to the west. Sometimes he swings up the winding road to the high circle on Round Top and pauses long enough to look over the valley that he has filled with industry and happy homes; but always before he starts for the main office in the Tannery building he drifts throught West Endicott.

As his car moves slowly along, George F. is looking right and left, enjoying the vistas of green lawns, the neat, well painted homes. Groups of children on their way to school see the car coming, and halt at the nearest curb. They all know the driver.

"Hello, George F.!" they sing out to him, smiling and waving their hands.

"Hello, youngsters!" he replies, with a flourish of his old gray cap, and slowly goes on his way to work.

CHAPTER EIGHT

A Panoramic View of the Valley

I HAD my first extensive view of the Susquehanna valley between Binghamton and West Endicott on May Day, 1934. To honor George F. Johnson, one hundred thirty thousand people of the region celebrated with a great parade as evidence of their friendship and esteem, while in other parts of the country there were strikes and fears of riot. The Endicott Johnson workers had planned the celebration for themselves, but all the neighbors asked leave to join them. All Broome County made holiday, with schools, shops and business generally at a standstill, while a vast procession of working men and women, with bands and banners and richly decorated floats, marched and cheered to testify their regard.

By special trains on two railroads and in endless streams of busses and automobiles, visitors came from far and near to join in the tribute to the man and the system that for forty years have brought prosperity to this region. Mayors and business men, teachers, and clergymen of all faiths were in the multitude; and eleven thousand workers from other local industries marched with the army of nineteen thousand Endicott Johnson workers. It was a spontaneous outpouring of friendly regard.

The gathering of so many thousands of people intent upon this purpose made a stirring spectacle. From early morning they were in motion, all wheels rolling toward the common centre of attraction, the reviewing stand at Endicott, six miles below Binghamton. For hours all the traffic on the roads seemed to move in that direction, as if drawn by an irresistible magnet.

Such was the inspiring occasion for my initial survey of the valley. The first thing to catch the eye was the festive dress of the city of Binghamton. Flags were fluttering on the public buildings and from the staffs of stores and dwellings on every side. Shop windows were bowers of red, white and blue streamers, and most of them exhibited a large portrait of Mr. Johnson and the greeting, "Welcome Home, George F.!" From the largest department stores to the smallest delicatessen shops and bootblack parlors, all joined in the display. In the windows of delivery trucks, busses, taxis and private cars bright stickers showed the picture and repeated, "Welcome Home, George F.!"

From a high hilltop on the west side of Binghamton there is a clear view for miles down the Susquehanna river, whose sinuous course marks the border between the states of New York and Pennsylvania. North and south of the stream ranges of tree-clad hills enclose the valley in a frame of living green. Much of the land is laid out in farms and sloping pastures, which look rich and well kept under the bright sun of a May morning. It affords a rural background for many groups of Endicott Johnson factories and tanneries and the clusters of workers' homes near at hand. Rising from the masses of steel, brick and concrete, with their myriads of gleaming windows, tall chimneys and their dark plumes of smoke dominate the picture.

The factories are most thickly grouped at Johnson City, on the outskirts of Binghamton; then another mass looms up, almost as large, at Endicott, five miles below. Closely adjoining lies West Endicott, not quite so thickly built up; and with a good glass one can see on the horizon the bulk of Owego, twelve miles distant, an old and thriving village of five thousand people, in which there is only one Endicott Johnson factory at the time of writing. Seen in perspective, these workshops of nineteen thousand persons seem to fill the right bank of the river, and it is only on a closer view that the many open spaces appear.

And the whole panorama differs from that seen in most industrial regions in two prominent features— the really handsome homes pressing close to the factories, and the great wealth of verdure, the trees and grass woven in and out among them in rich profusion. The dwellings looking out from their banks of leafage, and the shining river, like a long ribbon of silver unwinding, mingle in a pleasing prospect. One could be very homesick for this valley.

In the city of Binghamton, where, as we have seen, George F. arrived in 1881 with eight cents in his pocket, there are three Endicott Johnson shoe factories. The first is called the Busy Boys', and it makes only one line of shoes. It is a plain five-story structure, with no attempt at ornamentation except a dignified tower over the entrance and a lawn before the door. In this building, with half an acre of floor space, three hundred fifty workers fashion more than four thousand pairs of boys' Goodyear welt shoes every day. It overlooks the eight-acre Recreation Park, with George F. Johnson gave to the city in 1922, and was built at that time. It has abundant light and air from three hundred windows, one-third of which have a view of the park. A few workers have homes in the neighborhood, but not in such numbers as in the villages down the river, where there was more land when the company began to build factories there.

When the evangelist Billy Sunday finished his campaign of revival meetings in Binghamton, the tabernacle built for his services stood idle for a long time. It is a neat one-story building of brick, of attractive design, but not very well adapted to business purposes. When the Endicott Johnson company was looking for more factory space because of the increasing demands for boys' shoes of the Goodyear welt variety, Mr. Johnson suggested that they might use the tabernacle.

The company bought the building and named it the George F. Johnson Factory. They filled it with workers and machinery, in 1926, and ever since then the walls that used to echo the strains of Rodeheaver's trombone and Billy Sunday's exhortation for sinners to hit the sawdust trail have resounded to the whir and clank of machines. Three hundred people turn out thirty-six hundred pairs of boys' shoes a day. Not many of them live near the factory.

The Work Shoe Factory, built in Binghamton in 1932, makes strong, heavy shoes for mining and similar rough usage.

On the way out of Binghamton one is impressed by the beauty of a large church that stands on Main Street, as the broad, smooth highway is called all the way to Owego. The structure is of reddish brown stone, of modified Gothic design, with a lofty tower, and in its auditorium, lit with stained glass windows, two thousand worshippers find ample accommodation. Adjoining are the rooms for the various societies connected with the church. The edifice and its entire equipment were given to the Methodist Episcopal Church, in 1926, by George F. and C. Fred Johnson as a memorial to their mother, Mrs. Sarah Jane Johnson.

The stranger can hardly guess when he has crossed the city line, for the succession of stores and dwellings is unbroken. But where Johnson City begins, he comes to a lofty and massive arch of gray granite that spans the way from curb to curb. On it is carved in bold letters, "HOME OF THE SQUARE DEAL." On the keystone are the words, "Erected by E. J. Workers." They presented it to George F. Johnson in 1919.

The visitor cannot help contrasting the hustling town of today with the drowsy farm lands that stretched away on every side when George F. Johnson, in 1889, came here from Binghamton to pick out a site for the new factory of his employer, G. Harry Lester. Factories, banks, shops, parks, apartment houses, all the apparatus of crowded city life, are plentiful in this home of fifteen thousand industrious people.

Four blocks south of Main Street, on Corliss Avenue, is the Pioneer Factory, which Mr. Lester built in 1890, after clearing the fields of stumps and stone walls. It stands today as solid as when it was put up, a four-story red frame block, plain as a pike-staff but with plenty of windows and easy stairways. In itself it is unchanged, but its surroundings have changed many times.

After George F. Johnson took charge and the busi-

ness began to grow, new sections were added to the
Pioneer—a T-shaped extension in one place, an L in
another; then the arms of the T were carried out
until they ran the entire length of a city block; then
another building parallel with that, and various
spurs and cross-sections in between. The Pioneer and
its additions now occupy the whole city block, twenty
times as much area as in the beginning, with every
branch of shoemaking flourishing on its acres of
floors. Meanwhile the needs of the constantly growing business have called for the building of warehouses and factory after factory until they seem to
fill the whole region.

Near the old mother factory is the Pioneer Annex,
a handsome, six-story building of steel and white
concrete, erected in 1916, in more modern style, with
a broad, formal entrance, modestly ornamented, one
of the very few that depart from the severe simplicity
that generally prevails. The building looks like one
enormous window, its frame as slender as could be
made to hold so many hundreds of panes of glass. It
is called the Infants' Factory, and in it are made
baby shoes, from the tiny things that the very youngest brandish in their mothers' arms to the little shoes
that yearlings wear when they take their first steps.

Close at hand are the Scout Factory, a great red
brick building, erected in 1912 with three and a half
acres of floor space in its five stories, where they
make every day seventeen thousand pairs of long-

wearing, comfortable work and play shoes; and the Misses' and Children's Factory, of the same date, a plain four-story brick house, with a daily capacity of sixty-five hundred pairs of shoes of fashionable models. Sunrise and Jigger factories are near neighbors. They are industrial twins; for in the first factory they work all summer making every kind of rubber waterproof shoes for winter use, from lumbermen's pacs to the sandals that young women wear; and in the winter the whole crew shift over to Jigger and make basketball and tennis shoes and all other kinds of rubber-soled sport shoes that people want in the summer.

Seen in bulk, this mass of factories is overwhelming. They lie on either side of lines of railroad tracks and loading platforms, from which carloads of shoes are despatched to the company's warehouses and to wholesalers and jobbers, north, south and west. A broad margin of clear ground surrounds each factory, so that light and air have ready access to the buildings, and from many of them one can see trees not too far away. The shops are as clean and as hygienic as gymnasiums.

There is no attempt at landscape gardening around the factories in the Pioneer tract; for every inch of available space is paved with concrete and occupied by the cars of the workers, parked there all day. Those close-packed rows of cars, by the way, pleasantly shocked a committee of Soviet shoe men who visited the Endicott Johnson factories in 1934.

"All these belong to workers?" they exclaimed. "Impossible! In Russia only the officials have cars."

In the narrow streets near Pioneer you will see many workers' homes on small plots of ground. They are neat but crowded too close for comfort. They well illustrate the old order of things in the industrial world; for, as we know, when Mr. Lester built his new factory he bought acreage all around it, and sold lots to his workers at fancy prices. He made so much out of this that he branched out as a real estate dealer, and so began the speculations that ruined his business. Mr. Lester's workers eagerly bought his land and built these houses in the 1890's, to avoid the tedious trip from Binghamton by horse-car and the muddy walk from the city line—and Endicott Johnson workers still live in them.

But they are no more like the houses George F. Johnson and his brothers have built for their workers than a little old Model T car is like a modern sedan. Among these relics of a less enlightened age there is an old cottage that is always freshly painted white. It is the one George F. Johnson used to live in, and he never lets it suffer neglect.

Across the way from that cottage and not far from Pioneer stands the E. J. Workers' Hospital of Johnson City, a spacious three-story brick building, in which a staff of doctors and nurses treat ailments, from simple toothache or eye strain to those which call for delicate internal operations. A row of baby carriages near the door belong to mothers who have brought their infants to the well babies' clinic, where the little ones are weighed and examined and experts suggest any needed change that will help them grow stronger—the prevention idea you find all though the E. J. organization. On the same theory, workers are urged to visit the doctors, no matter how trivial they may think their troubles may be.

Within the block is the Wilson Memorial Hospital, an older establishment, named for the devoted doctor who founded it and given to the community by the Endicott Johnson company. Near it is the Nurses' Home, given to the people of Johnson City by C. Fred Johnson in memory of his wife. This is a handsome, big four-story structure of red brick and limestone, in which eighty nurses, some on duty in the hospitals and others in training, live among ideal surroundings, every bedroom open to sunlight, and with an immense drawing room.

Three blocks up the hill from the Pioneer tract is a big, one-story structure in the square, on which is displayed a sign, "E. J. Workers' Public Market." Here farmers from miles around bring their produce three times a week and sell it to the workers and their neighbors. All are welcome, on the E. J. principle of the greatest good for the greatest number, and on the outer wall is carved a motto borrowed from George

F. Johnson, "Live and Help Live." Facing the market is the tall red brick building of the E. J. Fire Prevention and Safety Department, in which sixty watchmen, firemen, signal operators, rescue men and an ambulance corps guard the welfare of workers, homes and factories, night and day.

Further west is C. F. J. Park, named for C. Fred Johnson, with playgrounds and tennis courts among the trees, on land reclaimed from dreary swamp and the wreck of a brickyard. In it is an immense swimming pool that contains a million and a half gallons of water from artesian wells, filtered and heated to a constant temperature of 72°. Its springboards and chutes tower high in the air. Across the street from it is George F. Pavilion, a broad, deep structure of steel and concrete in Spanish design, with a floor on which twelve hundred couples may dance. A park and garden surround the pavilion. The Endicott Johnson company pays all the expenses and gives the entire gross receipts to charities, about $50,000 a year.

But all these things are only part of the E. J. activities in Johnson City. Once more on Main Street, the visitor sees the institution known as Your Home Library, another Johnson gift to the citizens. It occupies a fine, roomy old mansion, built early in this century, when a big man felt he must have a big house to live in. His heirs sold it. It is set in the midst of an acre of grounds, with trees, thick green hedges and many flower beds to add to its charm.

Some of the littlest boys break a back window once in a while at their ball games, but the librarian never has them punished, remembering how George F. had to flee from the police when he broke windows playing ball. Your Home Library is well stocked, and its readers take out almost as many books of non-fiction as of fiction. It has a special children's room, with little people's furniture, books youngsters like, and a story-telling hour several times a week. It also serves as a community centre, with rooms for sewing classes, meetings and dances, and kitchens for those who like a bit of supper between dances.

North of Main Street, beside a well kept park, one sees a workshop which from a distance looks like a palace of snow and glass. It is really a six-story structure of steel and white concrete, with low, square towers, and pierced with six hundred windows. It covers an acre of ground, and it has been called the best equipped shoe factory in the world. Opened about the time of the Armistice that ended the World War, it was called the Victory Factory. Here are made twenty-two thousand pairs of shoes a day. Near it are scores of workers' homes, most of them of stucco or concrete, each with its bit of trim lawn, all sold at cost to the workers by C. Fred Johnson. The plots are small, for land has long been scarce at Johnson City.

Also facing the park is the C. F. J. Factory, named in honor of C. Fred Johnson. It is not quite so light in color as Victory and only five stories high, but it covers more space and produces twenty-four thousand pairs of shoes a day. Beside it is a two-story building, which houses one of the company restaurants. Its broad porches provide attractive resting places after meals. In it two thousand persons can lunch or dine at one time—for fifteen cents apiece.

Other E. J. factories in this region make up a group almost as large as those clustered around Pioneer. The adjoining park was created by the municipal authorities in memory of Harry L. Johnson, youngest of the brothers, who was for years the general superintendent at Johnson City. He died in 1922, deeply distressed because the post-war depression made it necessary for the company to reduce wages for a while. In the park is a bronze statue of Mr. Johnson, erected by thousands of workers, his friends. In the vicinity you will see eighty attractive homes he built for workers and sold to them at a loss of a thousand dollars on each house, rather than ask them to pay more than the first estimated cost.

There is another park not far away, named for C. Fred Johnson, who established it. It has a baseball diamond and athletic track and field, with a grand stand that seats five thousand people. Here the E. J. workers play ball and see the contests of the Tri-State League of professionals. The field is equipped with flood-lights for night baseball games and occasional boxing matches, with low prices of admission.

On the way out of Johnson City the visitor passes the homes of C. Fred Johnson and his son, Charles F., Jr. They are roomy, of substantial design, with no suggestion of luxury, and are surrounded by lawns, unfenced, with beds of flowers. Homes of workers are close by on either side. The visitor gets the impression that the E. J. idea of industrial democracy applies to living as well as working.

Down the highway to the westward one keeps the Susquehanna in view most of the time, placidly winding its way to the distant Chesapeake, a gentle, unhurried stream. There are many groves and an occasional house on its grassy banks. Farms are scattered along the way, and always the wooded hills rise on the northern and southern horizon. Five miles from Johnson City the environs of the incorporated village of Endicott begin, and the traveler presently is driving through broad streets, shaded with rows of luxuriant maple and birch trees.

The homes are of modest architecture of many types, the older ones of wood and the newer of stucco, and they all have the look of being well cared for, with no lack of paint. Around every one lies a good lawn, well trimmed and ornamented with shrubs and beds of flowers. Many have vines and gardens. Altogether they present an appearance of bourgeois prosperity and comfort which must have irritated the

Monument to George F. Johnson in Recreation Park, Binghamton. Erected by the citizens of Binghamton

Bolsheviks who came to town in 1931 and tried to stir up discontent until they were laughed away. There are several other industries besides shoemaking in Endicott, but here, as in Johnson City, most of the people are employed by the Endicott Johnson company.

Where Washington Avenue, the chief business thoroughfare, cuts across the highway, one finds at the left a long grand stand of steel and concrete, built on a steep hillside. There is room for six thousand spectators in it, and on the field below the Johnsons maintained a trotting track, where the Orange County races and many other big events were contested. This is En-Joie Park. When the depression gave the workers more leisure and opportunity for a keener interest in athletics, the company wiped out the track, in 1930, and gave over the entire thirty-six acres to sports for the workers, with cinder paths, baseball diamonds, and other facilities. In winter the ground is flooded for skating, and there are occasional championships as well as activities every day and evening for the shoemakers.

Within sight and hearing of the stand is the band pavilion, where concerts and vaudeville are given free all summer to thousands of people, many of them coming from distant towns. Beyond the pavilion is a grove for picnickers, with a dining hall in case of rain. Swings, a merry-go-round, a wading pool, a roller skating rink, and a crescent-shaped swimming pool that holds a million gallons of pure water, stand out among the many attractions that the Endicott Johnson company gives to the community free. The cost to the company is $30,000 a year.

From the Washington Avenue corner all Endicott lies in plain view. First one sees the high school, housed in a spacious red brick structure of modern design and surrounded by lawns and trees. Fronting En-Joie is a smaller park, in which stands the tall Memorial Monument with heroic statues in bronze, erected by George F. Johnson, in 1920, to honor the thirteen thousand Endicott Johnson workers who served during the World War, in the field and at home. On a tablet of bronze are carved the names of the dead. Across the street from the monument is the home of George F. Johnson, in the midst of a broad, smooth lawn, enclosed in low hedges of privet and adorned with many white birches.

The house is of frame construction, of generous size, in plain Colonial style, with a broad porch, well shaded, and it is painted in Colonial yellow tint. Wide beds of flowers surround it. Compared with the mansions of most captains of industry, this home of the chief of a $36,000,000 corporation is of Spartan simplicity. The establishment is a model of comfort, without a trace of show, a sort of big brother to the many E. J. workers' homes that lie close at hand. And it sets an example of thrift and neatness that you will see reflected all through the neighborhood.

To walk up Washington Avenue is to see Endicott in epitome, the home and workshop of twelve thousand busy people. The thoroughfare ends, half a mile away, in the mass of Endicott Johnson factories and tanneries, which, with their high roofs and towering smokestacks, seem a whole city in themselves.

First, is the immense Ideal factory. You turn the corner, and face two other factories, and the Upper Leather, the Chrome Leather and the Sheepskin tanneries on the right, with the Fire Prevention building in the foreground; while on the left are the Sales Building and its Annex, and the original Sole Leather Tannery, where the company began its first tanning on a big scale and George W. Johnson learned the business. In this building George F. Johnson and his son George W. have their offices. Nearer by, on the left, is the large three-story E. J. restaurant, where two thousand men and women can lunch at one time, with a food store on the ground floor.

Oak Hill Avenue, straight ahead, dives under the railroad and climbs the hill to the horizon. Along the streets east of it are the homes of hundreds of E. J. workers from Italy, Russia, Poland and Czecho-Slovakia. This is the North Side of Endicott. The homes are as neatly kept as any in the valley. The spire of St. Joseph's Catholic Church, high on Witherill Avenue, towers far above the rest, and there are two Russian Catholic churches, besides several of evangelical denominations. The Temple of the Sons of Italy is one of the finest buildings in town.

Back to Main Street now, where you pass the Ideal Home Library, housed in another great old mansion, given to the community by Endicott Johnson, which renders to this neighborhood the kinds of service that Your Home gives at Johnson City. A little way to the west you pass under another Square Deal Arch, which marks the village limits, erected by the workers at the same time as the Johnson City arch. Now you are in the village of West Endicott. In the midst of the village are the West Endicott, the Fair Play and the George F. Improved factories, the great house of the Fire Prevention Department, and in between are the playgrounds.

Climb the high hill called Round Top south of the village, and look around. Just below is the beautiful Ideal Hospital, given to the community by George F. Johnson, and the Nurses' Home, next door, given by Mrs. Johnson in memory of her sister. West of the hill lie the En-Joie Health golf links with the Susquehanna at its edge, on which thousands of E. J. workers play from the time the snow leaves until it comes again. To the north are farms, on some of which E. J. workers live. Below Round Top the village of West Endicott is spread, looking like some painter's dream of what an industrial community should be.

In the middle distance eastward is Endicott, its

factories, homes and schools blended in appealing contrast; and farther away the masses of Johnson City factories, ringed about with dwellings, tell the same story of people working and living in comfort. Swimming pools that gleam among the green of parks are the high lights of the picture. On every side the spires of churches appear as often as the stacks of factories. They are of all faiths, and the Johnsons have helped them all abundantly, regardless of denomination.

There is throughout the whole panorama a feeling of balance, of harmony, of unity of purpose. It is a symbol of what men working together can accomplish for their mutual good. More than a symbol, it is the visible, living proof of their achievement.

CHAPTER NINE

People at Work

WHEN the whistles in the twenty-nine Endicott Johnson factories, at seven in the morning, sound the beginning of another day, an army of men and women start the machines going. Through twelve miles of the Susquehanna valley, since half-past six, they have been on their way, in their cars, in busses and on foot. Each one has punched the time clock before the hour, for they are all on piece work except the clerks and laborers, and all are keen to earn as much as possible. Earning depends on the quality as well as on the quantity of their product.

When the whistles blow again, at four, they have added one hundred seventy-five thousand pairs of shoes, boots and rubber footwear to the world's supply, at the rate of three hundred sixty-five pairs each minute, during the day. Each man or woman has made, by united effort, from green hides, crude rubber and other raw stuff, eighteen shoes, as perfect as human skill can produce them; and the day's output, neatly packed, come sliding down the chutes to the shipping room.

This is the result of a highly organized system, based upon a spirit that leavens the whole body of workers—a fusion of friendship and fair play. The fruit of that spirit appears in the cheerful efficiency of the workers, and you catch an echo of it when you hear them speak of the chairman, the president and the vice president of the Endicott Johnson Corporation as George F., George W., and Charley.

There is no back-slapping or handshaking; there is just friendship and understanding. The idea that governs is: "See what you can make *of* the business, not make *out of* the business." George F. expresses it in his acts as in his words: "Live and Help Live." It satisfies everybody, from the oldest customer to the newest apprentice—and it pays dividends in money as well as in happiness.

The army of workers is made up of men and women of all ages and many races. The ages range from new graduates of the local high schools to gray-haired men and women forty years with the company and its predecessor. Most of them were born in the Susquehanna valley or in New England, among them many of Irish blood, but there are thousands from Italy, Russia, Poland and Czecho-Slovakia, to say nothing of small groups from other parts of Europe. This army, which increases at the rate of one thousand a year in good times, is recruited with the utmost care; for there is more at stake than merely hiring people who may stay a little while and then drift away. The company has steady work for steady people. Therefore most of those who come to look for jobs feel that they will get work which will last as long as they do it right, with help to buy good homes at low cost, with care for their health and the health of their families, besides provision for old age if they need it. In a word, an E. J. job is a career.

The applicant for a job first undergoes a thorough physical examination by a doctor of the Medical Relief. If he has no serious defect, he is put to work for six months on trial—after he has undergone another examination by the head of the personnel department, a psychologist, who has been with the company since 1924. He has a roomy office in the Sales Building at Endicott. Sometimes there is a line of a dozen or more, rarely fewer than four or five, waiting to interview him.

The job-hunter is as welcome as a customer, and he feels at ease in the friendly air of the office. The psychologist invites him to a chair, and they sit in for a friendly talk—about where he has worked before, what he would like to do now, and how long he would like to stay. If the applicant has had experience as a cutter or laster or in any other branch of shoemaking, the talk is simply a means of getting an impression of his character and his mental make-up; gives an opportunity to observe whether he is keen, alert, the kind of man who will do what he has to do for all he is worth.

If the applicant is a youngster just out of high school, he is asked what studies he liked best and how well he did in them. If he wants to learn the trade, the psychologist tries him with the modern apparatus of pegs and boards to test his mental grasp and dexterity. If he would like to be a cutter, he is tried at matching little models of patterns, to gauge his accuracy of vision, and faculty of quick and just comparison. If he wants clerical work, he is tried with the standard Thurston tests.

When workers fall below par, show that they are not geared for their jobs, it is the psychologist's business to find out what is the matter and to suggest a cure for the trouble. Often he discovers that they are better fitted for another kind of work, more profitable for them and for the company. In all cases the formal psychological examinations are not the chief means of judging capacity, but rather they are aids to a common sense sizing up of the man and his conditions.

One who looks for the first time at the miles of factories in operation is bewildered by a mass of movements that seem to be without plan or system. He sees lines of freight cars groaning and clashing up to the long platforms, the motor trucks that look like good-sized houses rumbling away with loads of big cartons of shoes. In between are the tanneries, quivering to the roll of giant cranes, which pick up a ton and a half of dripping raw hides at one time and swing them down into the vats, and the factories filled with people who move amid the whir of machinery and the clatter of conveyors.

Nothing could be more confusing to the stranger's sight and hearing—yet the whole business is moving forward in a smooth and well-planned program. The tanneries are near the principal factories, so that the leather they make need not be carried far; the shops that shape the findings and smaller parts are close to the shops that use them; the shipping rooms open upon the railroad loading platforms, so that the cartons of shoes can be quickly stacked in the cars, and the motor trucks swing up to their appointed places on the outer edge of the factories, only a few yards away from the main highway. From raw stuff to finished product, the progress is as orderly as the march of the seasons. What seems scattered at loose ends is really as compact as the parts of a great engine.

Here are twenty box cars alongside the Sole Leather Factory at Endicott, loaded with hides of Argentine steers, just off the ship at New York. Gangs of men slide the packs of wet and salty skins down to their powerful pony motor trucks and roll them away to the beam-house, where they are washed, scraped bare of hair and flesh—which are used for felt, glue, grease and fertilizers—then "bated," to make them ready for tanning. Within three weeks these sides of leather will be smooth, brown soles of shoes, on their way to the wearers. As fast as one train is emptied, another slips into its place. Not a moment is lost.

Another string of box cars—forty this time—stops at the platform. They are full of calfskins from the meat packing plants in Chicago, on their way to the beam-house for cleansing and bating. From there they go to the Calfskin Tannery next door, where, by the use of chrome liquors, they are quickly made into stout leather. Within a few days they will be parts of the endless stream of shoes. The outer sides, or grain leather, will be trucked over to Ideal Factory, across the way, or up to Johnson City, to be used as the uppers of everyday shoes; the inner layers, or split leather, sent to Binghamton for strong, heavy work shoes, or cut up into linings, pockets or gussets.

The raw material coming in and the finished shoes moving out pass each other in constant tides, all on a production schedule that moves without delay or undue haste. Through the dull periods of 1933 and 1934, when many shoe factories in New England and the West were shut down half the time, the E. J. people continued steadily at work throughout the year, with four full days every week in the worst times—and then not for long. This was due to the planning carefully thought out in advance, planning that covered every step from buying hides and rubber at the lowest cost to making shoes that look attractive and wear long, and pricing them at figures that help to sell them quickly.

All the large scale shoe manufacturers in this country use practically the same machinery, on which they pay royalties to the makers; so that part of the business is the same for all. The Endicott Johnson company does not profit by the use of any special machinery. But the zest with which the people go at their work counts for much. It is piece work at higher pay than in other places. The factories are laid out so as to supplement one another in compact groups. The rubber reclaiming plant, at Johnson City, for example, among its acres piled high with old tires, is convenient to all the shops using rubber. The Fibreboard Mill stands in a nest of factories which use the counters and other parts it makes. There is a Chemical Department in each manufacturing centre, to supply all the compounds for tanning leather and dressing shoes, besides a laboratory in which experts constantly test and improve the compounds.

The raw material is first handled on the factory ground floor—soles cut out with sharp dies under heavy pressure; uppers and linings cut by accurate workers on swift machines. On the next floor people begin to fasten the parts together, and so upward—always by automatic conveyors, which save time—to the top floor, where the last touches are put on. From there to the packing and shipping room on the

ground floor the shoes slide down chutes. Nothing
that can be done by machinery is done by hand. All
the branches of the business are meshed together as
snugly as the works of a watch. From George F.
Johnson to the newest beginner, everybody is searching constantly for some way to save a few seconds of
time in the operations. In 1934 each one of the nineteen thousand workers averaged one and a half pairs
of shoes more a day than each one of the seventeen
thousand workers in 1928.

Perhaps the greatest element in the success of the
concern is the content of the workers, their freedom
from worry, and their sense of responsibility. "Be
your own supervisor," George F. often urges them.
"Don't leave any flaws or loose knots in a shoe. Make
sure that when it leaves your hands it is perfect." By
these appeals to pride in good work and the satisfaction in the pay it brings, the workers are stimulated to
their best efforts. One superintendent, with his directors and assistants, fifteen in all, manages the work of
eleven hundred people. Inspiring all the activity is
the spirit of friendly coöperation, the spirit which
George F. expresses with the phrase, "Make your
people comfortable."

While most of the E. J. workers are of New York
State or British and Irish New England stock, fully
one-third of them are of foreign birth or the children
of immigrants. When the Memorial Monument to
the E. J. workers who served in the World War was

dedicated, in 1920, a group of girls in the costumes of twenty foreign lands took part in the ceremony. Among them were Italians, Spaniards, Russians, Czecho-Slovakians, Hungarians, Poles, Mexicans, Finns, Danes, Swedes and Japanese, a miniature Congress of Nations. In the E. J. shops, working side by side are men and women of Italy, Hungary and Czecho-Slovakia, countries long at odds with each other. But these workers seem never to think of racial differences as they keep the wheels turning.

They not only work in close touch, but they lunch beside one another in the company diners and play on the same teams in the various sports, all without a suggestion of friction. There has never been any trouble in the valley over Old World jealousies, none of the shedding of bad blood that has happened at times in other industrial centres. I have heard an occasional E. J. worker complain that "the company does too much for the foreigners." Evidently George F. has heard such talk, too; for, in a letter to the workers, in December, 1926, he wrote:

"Let's have done with this hypocrisy and cant about 'superior birth and breeding.' Let's understand first what an American is. He is what America is, a man who respects himself and others—not because he happened to be born in one particular place in the world, but because he has the American spirit.

"The question, then, is one of spirituality. If you want to be 'one hundred percent American,' be con-

siderate and tolerant, broad and liberal—God-loving
and man-loving. Then you will be 'one hundred percent American,' even though you happened to be
born in Africa. Without this, you won't be 'one
hundred percent American,' even though you and
your parents and grandparents and greatgrandpar-
ents were born on Beacon Hill."

The march of the leather from the tannery to the
finished shoe, mysterious and puzzling to the casual
onlooker, is as orderly as the growth of an apple
from the blossom to the ripe fruit. And, as each stage
of the apple's growth is watched and tended, so each
process in the making of an Endicott Johnson shoe is
jealously guarded by the man or woman who is building it. There is only one director to every fifty operators, and each worker is keen to make sure that his
part of the program is done to perfection. He has
pride in his job; he knows that the more good work
he does the more he earns, and he goes at it with the
zeal of a musician playing his part of a composition.
It is an important element of E. J. policy that every
worker shall be his own boss—which stimulates self-
respect and keeps down the overhead charge on every
shoe.

There are two hundred eighty-five distinct operations in the making of every shoe. These differ greatly
from one another, and require hundreds of different
techniques and machines. Each operator has his
special job and works at top speed. The soles are

stamped out with heavy dies that fill the factory with their thunder. On the floor above men are cutting out uppers and their linen linings with accurate machines. The linings are pasted in and sewed fast; then the uppers are trundled in a rack to the machines with which workers stick in and clinch the eyelets faster than you can count. Each lot consists of a dozen pairs, with a long tag tied to it, from which each operator clips off a pay coupon as he finishes his part of the task.

Now insoles of flexible leather are tacked by machinery on to the wooden lasts upon which the shoes are built, the rows all symmetrical, without the variation of a millimeter. The lasts are shaped to duplicate every size and model of foot, and when styles change they are thrown into the junk heap by thousands. They make good fuel. The next worker puts the upper and the soled last into a pull-over machine, which has a score of slim steel fingers that draw the upper smoothly down over the last and fasten it so that the insole can be attached. Next the bed-laster finishes the operation on a machine that pulls the upper snugly around the insole and tacks it on. Another machine pulls out the tacks before the soles are sewed on. Seventeen tons of tacks are used every day in the twenty-nine factories and thrown into the scrap heap, to be used again in making steel. Nothing is wasted.

The shoes are trundled to another machine, on

One of the floats in the May Day celebration, 1934

which the leather and counter are fitted around the heel part of the last. The stiffening in the counter—which many manufacturers buy from specialists—comes from the Fibreboard Mill, at Johnson City. Now the welt, the narrow strip of leather that runs all the way round the bottom of the shoe, is sewed on in another machine. One seam unites the welt, the upper and the lip that has been turned up in the bottom of the insole.

Next the shank, an accurately curved strip of metal or close-grained wood, is cemented on to the insole, to stiffen it and support the arch of the foot. The space in front of the shank is filled with a hot, damp paste made of cork shavings and a special cement. This waterproofs the leather and helps the shoe to hold its shape. When it dries, the insole, welt and outsole are coated with rubber cement, pressed together, ready to be sewed into a solid footing on the next machine. More than fifty-five hundred miles of thread are sewn into E. J. shoes every day.

Now the shoes go, one by one into the grasp of a machine that seems to think. One visitor called it a machine with a conscience. As it rocks the shoe back and forth, its heavy vibrating rollers bear down on the sole from different angles, and press it so firmly to the shape of the last that neither time nor weather can change its position. That is an extraordinary thing to watch, the rollers going over every inch of the sole, shaping, smoothing and anchoring it in its proper place, omitting no detail of anxious care.

A short trundle now to the heel-slugger, a machine that nails the heel-seat to the rear of the outsole. Does that and nothing more, for the next move is to the heel-loading and attaching machine. The heels, whether of leather or rubber, are fed one by one into the grasp of a steel hand, which holds each in its place in turn. The operator pulls a lever, and the twenty or thirty nails that make fast the heel are all driven home in one movement. The shoe is at last a shoe.

Another machine grips it while emery wheels smooth and scour off all rough edges, and in still another machine the edge-trimmer trues up the edges of the soles. Still another trims the heels. Liquid is applied all around the edges, and a burnishing machine polishes them. After the bottoms have been sanded off smooth, the lasts are pulled out, and the shoes are snugly fitted on trees, polished and lightly ironed, to make sure there shall not be a wrinkle. Buffing and brush wheels put the last touches on soles and uppers; the shoes are inspected for possible blemishes, and the name of the dealer is stamped on. Retouchers and finishers pass on every shoe before it slides down a chute to the packing room, to be placed by pairs in boxes, ready for shipment in the big cartons.

The sounds and the speed of all the operations are

confusing to a stranger. He feels dizzy at the sight of such intense industry on the whirring, clanking machines. The air, with its smells of cements and dressings, quivers with thousands of mingled noises; the floor vibrates from the constant thud of metal on metal and the rumbling of the racks in which swarms of apprentices are wheeling dozens of pairs of shoes from one machine to the next in ceaseless streams. Near by and overhead, conveyors are in constant motion, carrying shoes to the next floor above, to be put through the next process.

Through all this welter of sound and motion, the tireless workers keep up the pace for hours—you should see them on the ball field or in the swimming pool after four o'clock—and even find time for a bit of talk or a few bars of song now and then.

To keep all of these diverse operations running smoothly and swiftly, without errors that would spoil the comfort or wearing quality of the shoes, is a big undertaking, but spirit and system do it. Do it with a quiet, ceaseless vigilance that gives the appearance of ease. The workers like to carry on that way. The philosopher who said that no salary would be big enough for the president of a company who could inspire his employees to want to do their best, would enjoy watching the E. J. people at work.

To begin with, they all know that the Johnsons have all learned the business from the bench upward, and could hold down jobs today. They know the trade and speak the language. The Johnsons live with their people, work, play, worship, rejoice and sorrow with them in a community of interest that is rare in the world of industry. They never preach about the dignity of labor. Instead, they act so as to make labor attractive, and they inspire a pride in workmanship that keeps the army of nineteen thousand eager to do their best at all times.

This they do by occasional letters from George F., on the bulletin board beside the time clock and on the Workers' Page; also by a more powerful argument:

Every promotion in the business is made from the ranks.

That has been the practice from the beginning. Every chief, from the officers of the corporation to the superintendents and directors and assistant directors of departments, has begun by working at the bench or in the vats, and earned his steps upward by his industry and his skill. In stimulating zeal this rule of action is as effective as Napoleon's reminder that every soldier carried a field marshal's baton in his knapsack. Outsiders are welcome to come in at the bottom of the structure; never as directors, for George F. says no self-respecting man would stand for it. Day by day the workers see their companions stepping up; therefore they work and think so that they can step up, too.

It has happened occasionally that a man promoted

above his fellows has been so intoxicated with power that he began to be arbitrary with them, even harsh. One case comes to mind:

A laster who received an order from a new assistant director began to question him about it, and the new man shut him off by saying, "If you don't want to do what I'm telling you, you can go take a little run and jump into the river!"

Many a man has answered a word like that with a swift right to the jaw; but this laster, though he was a husky with a very quick right, had a wit that was quicker yet. He knew that, no matter what the provocation, if he started a row that would throw a whole floor into confusion and stop the work of five hundred men for ten or fifteen minutes, it might cost him his job. He also knew something that helped him still more to control his temper—that the E. J. system would never allow anyone to abuse a worker. So without a word he turned to his work, and when the director of the department came near, stopped long enough to tell him all about it.

"Don't fret," the director told him. "Pete's new now, but he's a good fellow, and he'll be all right after he's broken in. I'll take care of him."

At lunch time the director and his assistant were side by side in the long line at the lunch counter. When they had filled their trays, the director led the way to a small table in a far corner, and the two sat down together, talked about the order they were putting through that day and half a dozen other things. Then quite casually the director remarked, "When you're doing all you know how to hurry stuff through, isn't it tough to find a fellow who'll want to give you an argument—"

"That's right," said Pete. "I had a dumb one this morning—"

"Well, you let him talk it out and get it off his chest," said the director. "Makes him easier in his mind, and he'll do his work better. You know what George F. says—it's up to us to prove that we're the best friends the fellows have got on our floor. And we've got to prove it if we want things to run right. See what I mean?—no crabbing, but give 'em a boost whenever you can."

That quiet little talk sobered Pete, and he became quite human. But if he had kept on as he had begun he probably would have been transferred to another factory. Arbitrary bossing does more harm than sand in the machinery, and the Johnsons never tolerate it. If that laster, or any others on his floor, felt that they were being abused by the new man, they would tell the superintendent about it, and if the abuse continued, any one of them or a group of them would drop in for a talk with one of the Johnsons. Then there would follow a searching investigation that would bring out the facts and a fair decision on the facts.

There is no such thing as a "shop committee" in all

the Endicott Johnson establishment, and there never has been. Though some employers have adopted that system as a cure for dissatisfaction, the idea has never appealed to George F. Johnson—"Too much red tape in it," he says. "Too much static between us and the men."

Every man or woman in the Endicott Johnson factories is his or her own committee, and anyone with a grievance is invited—invited, not permitted—to go to the head of the concern and state that grievance. The door is always open. That has been the rule from the beginning. The humanity of it, the satisfaction it gives, is a big contribution to the success of the Endicott Johnson Corporation.

Each factory and tannery is run by a superintendent, who is responsible for all that goes on—not only to turn out the product required in first class shape, but to see that the workers are comfortable and contented. He is aided by a director at the head of each department, and they in turn by their assistants. Endicott Johnson has no use for foremen.

"Too much boss idea in a foreman," George F. says. "We have directors, who guide the workers, help them when they need help, and see that they do their work right. The director does not try to drive them. Anyone who works with us needs no driving. He knows we are all trying for the same thing—to do a good job because it's worth doing well—and he does his share. If he doesn't catch the idea, doesn't do his best, he'll probably be happier somewhere else, and we'll not try to hinder him from going. And anyhow men are much better employed making shoes than trying to make lazy fellows work."

George F. has a letter on the Workers' Page— that unusual meeting place for all the E. J. family in the Binghamton *Sun*—once in a while on this subject. Usually it is in response to someone who has written him anonymously, complaining that he is working too hard and asking why he can't be put on weekly pay, so he can take it easier. The fact is that all the workers I have seen in a dozen visits to these factories, row after row of them at their machines, looked alert, intent upon their business, and cheerful. The speed that seemed blinding to strange eyes was an old story to them, familiar from much repetition. Their eyes keenly watched every movement of the shoe in the machine, kept it adjusted to the line it must follow, but they were able to exchange a few words now and then with a neighbor, especially when they were clipping off the pay coupon from a long tag after finishing their special part of a dozen shoes.

One girl in Ideal Factory seemed to be burning herself up with intent devotion to her work. She was tall and slight, eighteen or so, with features exquisitely clear, and large, dark eyes that had a feverish lustre—or so they appeared. As her slim fingers flew back and forth with a swiftness that would make a pianist's fingers look slow, she was frowning in her deep concentration on her task.

"Poor thing," I said to myself in passing. "She won't last long at that pace." But, on returning from the other end of the room, I saw the same girl—and could not believe that she really was the same. She was telling something funny to the girls next to her, her eyes dancing with merriment, the frown gone from her smooth brow, her white teeth flashing in a charming smile, while her slim fingers were flying fast as before. She needed no one's pity.

Another girl I saw, at Johnson City, was putting laces in tennis shoes, and her hands moved with such speed that the eye simply could not register their movements. She laced a dozen shoes in a few seconds. She was smiling, too, and seemed to do it all without effort.

Bigger earnings from piece work inspire the cheerful activity of these workers, and besides George F. never misses a chance to tell them all how much fairer the piece system is than pay by the day. He published in the E. J. Workers' Review, February 20, 1920, a speech he made to the E. J. carpenters at their get-together supper in the Endicott Diner.

"It is a common thing," he said, "to see carpenters gossiping, lolling around, yapping, smoking, time-killing. I don't blame you for this. It's the rotten system under which you have been working, and it is degrading in the extreme. You haven't any incentive to do better, so why should you try to do better? The day system is rotten as hell, through and through."

Mr. Johnson compared this with the advantages of pay for actual work done.

"Under the piece system, in one of our factories," he said, "we have cutters earning seventy dollars a week—no overtime, either. We have other cutters, under the same system, same wages, same conditions, same leather, earning forty dollars a week, and we have cutters earning not even forty dollars.

"The man who earns seventy dollars represents an investment in machinery and factory space of little more than half what the other fellow, who can earn only forty dollars, represents. He doesn't take up any more room; it doesn't take any more power to produce light, heat and power for him—takes a smaller investment in capital. If every man in the business was like the seventy dollar a week man, it would take only about two-thirds as much room, two-thirds as much machinery, light, heat and power, to produce the same number of shoes. The difference is in the men.

"The man who earns good wages is alive. It is just as natural for him to move that way as it is for the other fellow to move slowly. His mind is quicker. His muscles are more attuned to the activities. He is worth more to himself, to the company, and to the world. Such a difference as that doesn't exist among day workers, does it?

"What has happened in our cutting department is this: the man who is earning forty dollars now would not be earning more than thirty dollars if the other man didn't inspire him. If there were no seventy dollar man, there wouldn't be the forty dollar man. He would have been a thirty dollar man—and the other would have been only a fifty dollar man perhaps. It is the desire and the will to try and do better, due to example. But this is lacking in day work. Quite the reverse is true. Someone is getting as much as we are who isn't doing half as much as we are. Consequently we slow up, and the cost of houses goes kiting, and the poor men who live in the houses pay for this wasteful system.

"So now, who pays? Of course, the poor man. Capital does its own figuring, and capital figures in all the cost. Capital knows how to figure. They never neglect even interest charges. The cost is handed on to your poor neighbor, perhaps to you, and the whole system grows worse and worse. The tolls grow greater —and the poor man always pays."

How the E. J. workers thrive on piece work and the eight-hour day was shown in a statement published by the company in the Binghamton *Sun* on March 20, 1934. The average weekly wages in the shoe industry during 1933 in the States of Illinois, Missouri and New York were furnished and attested by Isador Lubin, Commissioner of Labor Statistics of the United States Department of Labor, at Washington. The Endicott Johnson average wages during the same year were furnished and vouched for by George F. Johnson. He pointed out that E. J. workers comprise three-fourths of the shoemakers in the State of New York, and that their pay raises the average for the state.

Here are the figures:

1933	ILLINOIS	MISSOURI	NEW YORK	E. J.
January	$9.01	$11.67	$17.51	$20.14
February	10.76	12.85	18.09	20.20
March	10.38	11.56	16.93	19.07
April	9.04	11.30	18.19	20.96
May	9.92	12.65	20.60	24.61
June	12.78	14.29	21.70	26.28
July	12.47	14.43	23.30	27.73
August	13.81	16.14	23.18	26.36
September	14.96	16.28	23.69	27.75
October	12.82	15.94	22.58	26.32
November	9.56	13.82	22.02	25.62
December	12.06	15.23	21.69	25.02
Average weekly pay per worker	11.46	13.84	20.79	24.17

Everything possible is done that will add to the comfort and efficiency of the workers. The E. J. restaurants that stand close to all the factories are open from six in the morning until after supper time. Some of the workers prefer to get breakfast in them rather than bother with it at home. Everyone has an hour off at midday for luncheon, but there are some who like to get a snack in the afternoon besides. They are welcome to it.

"I don't see," an efficiency expert said to George

F. Johnson, "how you can let your people take time out for eating in work hours. Bad for discipline, and sets an example of slackness. We keep our people on the mark all the time."

"Oh, I don't know," Mr. Johnson replied. "If a man works better on a full stomach, it's better for him and better for us to have him get something to eat. We don't have to prod our people to work. They like it. And the few minutes a man takes to satisfy his appetite he more than makes up with his comfort and contentment when he comes back to the job."

The easy-going policy does not mean any let-down in the pace at the machines. Work when you work and play when you play is the rule. But it is applied with fair consideration of the wishes of all. When the brief season for shooting pheasants began, in the fall of 1934, every man with a gun was eager to go out on the first day, for after that the birds would be very shy. There is good shooting in the hills that border the valley, and most of the workers are sportsmen. How they got their wish appears in the letter Charles F. Johnson, Jr., the vice president in charge of operations, wrote on October 25th of that year.

"To the Endicott Welt Workers: We have had petitions from some of the factories, requesting that we close down Monday, October 29—opening day for pheasants.

"Presumably a great many of our workers are anxious to go into the woods on Monday. They propose that we close Monday and work Friday, which would give them four days, same as though they worked from Monday to Thursday night.

"We are glad to comply with this reasonable request. We hope you will have a good time, with good weather, and that no one will be shot up."

The Endicott factories were running on a four-day week at the time. The change of schedule may have been awkward for some of the workers, but the majority of them wanted it, and the majority got it —another instance of the rule of the greatest good for the greatest number. No need to ask whether the cheerful coöperation of the vice president met with a hearty response from the sportsmen, or whether Tuesday's production sheets showed a big increase.

CHAPTER TEN

People at Work

THE Johnsons and other executives of the company all go to work at seven in the morning—even the treasurer, the auditor and the members of the legal department. There is no exception. George F. believes that all exemptions from general duties are unjust and do a great deal of harm. So he is working in his office at home at seven every morning, answering letters that come to him by the score, and replying to letters from the workers first of all. He is chairman of the board of directors.

His son, George W., president of the corporation, is at his desk, too, in the plain, old-fashioned general office in the Sole Leather Tannery at Endicott, at the same early hour. And in the Sales Building near by, Charles F. Johnson, Jr., vice president, is at his desk when the morning whistle blows. George F.'s brother, C. Fred Johnson, ruddy-cheeked and bright of eye, in charge of building and safety operations, is at his office, in the Fire Prevention building, Johnson City, or out supervising the newest factory under construction. He is eighty and looks sixty.

If a consultation is needed, the three chief executives gather in the general office at Endicott, or its duplicate at Johnson City—driving their own cars, by the way. Why waste three good men's time playing chauffeur when they might be making shoes? As soon as the conference is ended, each chief drives back to his own office, or to some factory where a new problem has come up. George W. gives special attention to the tanneries and their needs; Charles F., Jr. to the factories, and George F. to all that is going on.

Nobody knows at what moment George F. may step out of his roadster and drop in at any factory between Binghamton and Owego, to see for himself how the workers are thriving and how production is moving. He calls these visits fault-finding trips, but seeing him in a factory you would never think he is finding fault. Any changes he may suggest will be proposed at the general conference. He steps briskly along, and his glance takes in every movement in the vast room, keen, concentrated, missing no detail. Now and then he meets an old friend who worked beside him years ago, nods to him and says hello without interrupting his inspection. If he meets the same man a few hours later, at a picnic or a clambake, that is a different story. Work is out and play is in, and they eat clams, drink their beer and swap

Lasting room, Jigger Factory, Johnson City

yarns about the old days and what they are doing now.

On one of the inspection trips, in 1920, Mr. Johnson found an old companion of the Pioneer days busy at the edging machine, and told him it was high time he laid off and took life easy. The man said he'd think of it as soon as his youngest boy came out of high school. That was all for the moment, but on his next visit Mr. Johnson stopped again beside his old friend.

"Look here, Bill," he said, "I don't want to see you around this place any more. You turn in your coupons and go home—but call at the pay window every week, and you'll find a full envelope waiting for you."

On his inspection trips, in the summer of 1934, Mr. Johnson saw a few workers here and there who seemed a little listless, not quite up to par. He wrote a letter to all the workers, on July 12, which was put up beside the time clocks, on the restaurant bulletins and published on the Workers' Page.

"There is no feeling," he wrote, "except positive illness that is so disagreeable and hard to overcome as monotony. We have been questioned a great many times, why we have all our work, so far as humanly possible, based on piece work? Many who are unable to keep up and earn as much as some of their roommates, think a day system is better. But the truth is that the day system is the most monotonous and tiresome possible to devise—to say nothing of its un-fairness.

"To know in the morning that your compensation is fixed; to know that you must do the same thing all day long, to know that whether you do a little more or a little less, whether you are more or less interested and more or less efficient, your pay is automatically fixed—creates the most deadly monotony that I can believe possible.

"I have known this from experience. I worked as a day worker; and later as a piece worker I found I had more interest in my work. I was inclined to accomplish more and thus earn more. I then realized for the first time, how much more interesting and how much less monotonous my task was under the piece plan than the day plan of computing wages. The same person on the same job will do from one-third to one-half more work under the piece plan than he will under a fixed price, or so-called day system.

"An equally important point is the fact that you are interested in trying to produce, and therefore have overcome in part the deadly monotony of doing the same thing over and over, each hour, each day and each week.

"I have a further recommendation to make, that will relieve monotony and create more content and happiness: Become interested in the quality of your work. Trying to excel in that adds another incentive, and further relieves monotony and deadly dullness.

"Our chief need in life is someone to make us do our best.

"Competition is keen and growing keener. The fight for business is severe. We must please the eye, attract interest, fit the foot and create good wear. I know you desire, first of all, uniformly steady work, which increases the yearly income, vitally important to you and your family. Broken time means a loss to you. Lost time is never made up. It is gone forever. Opportunities thus lost to us are never to be regained.

"Interesting yourself in the quality of your work helps to create a superior product and consequently better sales, better wages, more happiness and decidedly less monotony in our daily task. I recommend as a cure—at least a help—to relieve dull, monotonous labor, keen interest in the quality of the work, resulting in a better finished product; hence the best way to secure better wages.

"It is very important and necessary, first, to attend strictly to your work. Interest yourself in the quality and the quantity, and thus help yourself to a better existence, more happiness, greater pleasure. Work is just as necessary for our health and well being as play—entirely apart from the income we derive from it. Both give us healthy exercise, to keep our minds and bodies fit.

"If you disagree with me, try to convince me that I am wrong, and we will have a little argument over the matter on the Workers' Page, for the benefit of the workers."

Apparently no one disagreed; for no one wrote to contradict the theory.

At the call of the noon whistle, hundreds of workers drift out of the factories into the E. J. restaurants, all conveniently near. They take their time; for the fire regulations, strictly enforced by patrolmen all day long, forbid smoking in any factory, and many a man lingers to puff a cigarette as he goes. For fifteen cents you get a choice of meat or fish, or varying kinds and styles of cooking every day, two good helpings of vegetables, often a salad, bread and butter, dessert or cake or pie or fruit, and choice of tea, coffee or milk—all of the best in the market, well cooked in home-made fashion and temptingly served in blue plate style. No dinner pail, even in its fullest days, could compete with this hot and appetizing meal.

These restaurants are examples of democracy in action. No places are reserved, and, as the lines form on the way to the serving counters, the superintendent of a factory or the president of the company takes his turn with the rest. The upper floor of each restaurant is a cafeteria, where a greater variety of dishes can be had at a little higher price. In both dining rooms there are long tables, scrupulously clean and neat, with a few small round tables in the corners. Day after day I have lunched well in the Endicott Diner and enjoyed the sights there.

At a long table near the west end of the room the vice president sits, with a superintendent, or a salesman back from the road, an auditor and others near him, talking about business as the meal is ended and the cigars begin to glow. Perhaps an attorney or the head of the distribution department is in the group. Close alongside at the same table, which holds forty or more, sit workers fresh from the machines, many of them in shirt-sleeves, all talking with one another as if they were at home. If in coming in or going out the vice president sees a familiar face, he nods, says, "Hello, Bill," and gets a friendly hello in reply. The scene is like that at the training table of a football team or a crew. There is the same friendly air, the absence of formality. After luncheon the workers stroll off in groups. They have fifteen or twenty minutes of leisure before they go back to the machines.

In all industries there are men who are not getting the best results because they do not fit their jobs and are better adapted to other work. To discover the trimmer who would be better off as a laster or cutter, or the stitchers who could earn more in some other department, is one of the jobs of the E. J. Personnel Department, which was instituted in 1924. Every applicant for a job is examined there before being hired, but adjusting workers who do not fit their tasks is equally important, not only for the comfort and prosperity of the worker but in the important saving of labor turnover.

An industrious tanner and his wife, a stitcher, had saved $3,000, but they needed more to go into business, in which they hoped to make more money. The wife suffered a paralysis of the right arm, which kept her from work; and, though the doctors did all they could for her, she did not improve after three weeks' treatment. The problem was put up to the psychologist at the head of the personnel department. He found that the woman had continued to work after her second child was born, leaving the baby in care of a nurse girl. The baby died, and the mother thought the death was due to her neglect. She wanted to stay home and take care of her older child, who had a bad cold, but her husband insisted she must keep on in the factory. The psychologist soon concluded that the paralyzed right arm was really caused by a subconscious defence mechanism.

He was able to clear this up by a simple oral discussion—sound medicine and sound applied psychology. Then he explained to the husband that his wife's arm was all right now, but that if she went back to stitching it would be paralyzed again. He let her stay home.

A side-laster who went to work on a strange machine began to have a backache every afternoon; soon he had it all day. He consulted the doctors, who gave him medicines and prescribed massage, but the pain became chronic, lasted all of one year. The psychologist went into the shop and saw that the side-laster, a short, stocky man, had to raise his arms uncomfortably high in order to work the machine. So he put a little platform under him—no more pain.

A girl who was not very speedy on the stitching machine became so discouraged that she was going to quit. She thought the other girls were racing with her and laughing at her for being so slow. The psychologist had her machine moved down to a corner, where she could work with her back to the rest. Her work improved, and so did her spirits, and in a few weeks she did as well as the average.

Endicott Johnson is neither an open shop nor a closed shop, as those terms are used technically. There is no labor union in any of them, though George F. Johnson has often said that he has no objection to anyone's joining a union if he likes.

"Most of the improvement in workers' hours, wages and working conditions have come from the efforts of workers' unions," he said to me, "and they have been the result of hard struggles. We don't believe that men should have to fight for decent treatment, and we have always tried to give them that, with maybe something more.

"When the unions of Binghamton held a big labor parade, in 1916, they invited us to parade with them, and they put us at the head of the line—thousands of our workers, with George and Charley marching with me at the front. Sam Gompers told me years ago, that we had already given our workers more than any union could ask, and that the Federation of Labor had more important work to do than to try to organize our people. John Mitchell told me the same thing. Jerry Ryan, union organizer of Binghamton, said the same thing. Our workers know that we are the best labor leaders for them—their interest is our interest always."

When the war demand for shoes greatly increased the business, in 1916, George F. Johnson raised wages and urged his partners to reduce the working day from nine and a half hours to eight. Mr. Endicott and the other conservatives reluctantly agreed to the wage raise, but they could not see any advantage in shorter hours. This was the period when, as George F. described it, "the country was on a huge drunk, everybody making money and millionaires being made over night." Yet he found it difficult to persuade the majority of his partners that it would be wise to adopt the eight-hour day. After much debate they consented, and on October 13, 1916, George F. wrote to the workers:

"The notice of an eight-hour working schedule, effective November 1st, posted in our tanneries and factories today, means much to many people. If progress, much talked about, means anything worth while, it must of necessity be applied to the lives of working people.

"We think we have made the lives of many thousands of people happy today, but we have also found that we have made this the happiest day of our own lives—a dream long dreamed come true. Easing the working conditions of a lot of faithful, loyal employees is worth while, and is a mighty good day's work."

There were more smiles to the square yard that morning in the E. J. tanneries and factories than anyone had ever seen there before. It looked as if everyone was congratulating himself and congratulating his friends. At lunch time groups gathered near all the E. J. diners, and men and women told one another that they ought to do something about this great surprise. Someone said he thought it would be a good thing to march down to George F.'s house after the whistle blew, at half-past five, and tell him what they thought of him. A hundred voices cried, "That's right. We'll go." All afternoon men were telephoning from one factory to another, arranging to meet at Main Street and Washington Avenue, Endicott, and line up for the parade.

Mr. Johnson was pleased when he heard of the movement, and he had only one suggestion to offer. The campaign that resulted in the reëlection of President Wilson was then at its height, and everybody knew that Mr. Johnson was in favor of Wilson; but he wanted to avoid anything that might look like a political demonstration. "Ask the people," he told his son George, "not to wear any campaign buttons. This is our own family party, and there's no politics in it." So the word was passed everywhere, and when the workers assembled there was not a political emblem in sight.

In the last twenty years there have been many "George F. Days" and "George F. Parades" in the valley, but none of them developed more enthusiasm than this. There were twelve thousand E. J. workers at that time, and every man and woman, boy and girl marched, eight abreast, before the porch, where George F. stood smiling at them and waving his hand, calling one friend after another by name as he passed. The close-packed ranks cheered as they came near him, and as they caught his eye, and still cheered as they moved by.

There were many American flags in the procession, and many placards hastily improvised, with slogans the workers composed, and men in the shipping department, handy with the brush, painted on big squares of cardboard used to make the cartons in which boxes of shoes are packed. One of the biggest was:

We Are Power: We Are Success,

Through Our Leader, the Great George F.

The idea made up for the strained rhyme. Others were:

Eight Hours' Work, Ten Hours' pay.

How Do We Get It? The Big E. J.!

We Can Work Ten Hours, but We Don't
Have to.

The tanners had a special motto, lettered in brown extract of tannin:

We Propose to Tan Shirkers' Hides.

That night the twelve thousand workers appointed a committee of one hundred eight men and women, representing every branch of the industry, to draft a letter of thanks to the Endicott Johnson company. It was:

"From the beginning, a quarter of a century ago, we have realized that the big, broad Endicott Johnson policy was founded on the sincere desire to have their people work and live under conditions that make for health, contentment, prosperity, and above all for the making of better men and women.

"All through the upbuilding of the immense organization, to which so many of us are indebted for our splendid opportunities, never once have they faltered in their wish to extend a helping hand. Some of us are privileged to know how much distress has been relieved by the ever-willing hearts of the real men who are the firm of Endicott Johnson and company.

"Their public benefactions, although modestly given, are well known. Always they have listened kindly to any grievance, real or fancied. And the fact that there has never been a ripple of labor disturbance in Johnson City or Endicott is a splendid testimonial to their keen sense of fairness toward their 'big family.'

"The unsolicited and voluntarily given eight-hour day calls forth our sincere thanks and appreciation, and on behalf of the big Endicott Johnson family we extend our heartfelt gratitude to our friends and employers, Messrs. Endicott Johnson and Company."

The committee a few days later published this letter, signed with their one hundred eight names, as a full page advertisement in the Binghamton *Sun,* and paid for it out of their own pockets, at regular advertising rates.

The workers showed their appreciation by going at the job with more vim than ever. And the enthusiasm lasted. Everybody watched the production figures for months after the change, and the records showed a sustained increase over the production records made under the nine-and-a-half hour schedule.

It is curious to note that two years later, the National Industrial Conference Board investigated the shoe industry and declared that "maximum efficiency is impossible under less than a fifty-two hour week." That was the spirit of the times, and the success of the Endicott Johnson experiment could not change it.*

*(Research Report Number 7, 1918; pages 50-52).

CHAPTER ELEVEN

Selling One Hundred Seventy-Five Thousand Pairs of Shoes a Day

THE one hundred seventy-five thousand pairs of shoes the Endicott Johnson workers produce daily would provide a new pair every day for each man, woman and child in the city of Grand Rapids. That means, with a five-day week, a total of forty-five and a half million pairs in a year of two hundred sixty working days, a mountain of shoes that the imagination can hardly comprehend. Beside it the Empire State building would look small. Yet that vast mass is distributed regularly and evenly by the Endicott Johnson Sales Department, always without stoppage and very seldom with any slowing down.

Without swift distribution of their product, the nineteen thousand shoemakers would have to quit work. There would be no pay envelopes, parks, playgrounds, hospitals or homes. Throughout New England and the West, in 1921, 1933 and 1934, many shoe factories had to shut down for long lay-offs because they could find no outlet for their product. Thousands of their workers were idle; while the Endicott Johnson workers went steadily on, busy five days a week, under the NRA plan during the latter two years.

Endicott Johnson's Sales Department has kept pace with the growth of the company, and promoted it, largely because George F. Johnson has put into it as much planning and drive as he has devoted to buying and tanning hides and making shoes. He is a born trader, and he has improved with practice. The same instinctive flair for salesmanship that enabled him to give the beginning firm of Endicott, Johnson and Company its first big increase in selling, inspires the sales organization still. The new firm was selling one thousand pairs a day to jobbers, which was the prevailing practice in 1900, as it had been for many years. The restless discontent with things as they are that drove George F. to look for better methods when he was a boy and which has inspired him ever since, caused him to go out on the road and sell more shoes than two men had been able to sell.

Soon he had a stronger incentive—some of the biggest jobbers began, in 1903, to build factories and sell shoes of their own make, giving them the preference over all others. The two new salesmen had an uphill job. Endicott, Johnson and Company's sales dwindled badly, and seemed likely to shrink further. The partners spent many anxious hours, trying to figure some way of escape from this dangerous situation.

"There's no reason why we can't sell direct to the retailers," said George F. at last. Mr. Endicott was doubtful about trying a thing that never had been done, but he remembered the big impetus his partner had already given to sales, and at length agreed with him. The firm made careful preparation before starting their revolutionary program. They selected a group of thirteen lively salesmen, had them study the various lines of E. J. shoes—many had been added to the original stogy boots and work shoes—and showed them how much cheaper they were than other makers' shoes of like quality. Also they began an extensive advertising campaign in the shoe trade journals that retailers would see.

Their slogan was "From Hide to Retailer," and they spread it from coast to coast, showing the retailer how much he could save by buying from a manufacturer who tanned his own leather, thus cutting out the profit that other makers had to pay the tanners. He could now save, too, the profit which ordinarily went to the jobber—another big item. Still, the advertising was conservative, on the side of understatement rather than making extravagant claims. It stressed the advantage of having every process directed by men who had risen from the bench, who had the practical knowledge that comes from long experience. It told of the fine leather E. J. made, smooth and long lasting, and of the good style of their shoes.

The retail trade became aware that a new element had come into the shoe business. And when the thirteen salesmen started out with their cases of sample shoes, they found the owners of shoe stores not only willing but eager to see what they had to offer. Wherever they went they sold big orders, and soon Endicott, Johnson and Company found their business increasing so fast that they had to build extensions on some of the factories to make room for more workers. They also built the Upper Leather Tannery at Endicott, in 1905, so that they could provide enough material to keep up with the orders that poured in. More traveling salesmen were added to the staff, and they brought in still more customers.

The new selling plan was a big step forward in the development of Endicott Johnson. It did much more than bring in a flood of orders from independent retailers. Their sales showed Endicott Johnson shoes so popular that their competitors, the regular dealers who bought through jobbers, had to carry more of them to meet customers' demands, in quality as well as price. So that from jobbers and independents both, orders came in so fast that the company could hardly keep up with them, even with more workers and factory extensions. As soon as they caught up, they began to manufacture, in advance,

Stitching room, Jigger Factory, Johnson City

stocks of the most popular models, to be ready for quick shipment to retailers.

The business grew so rapidly that every bit of space that could be used for storage was crowded. The company developed new lines each season, from improvements in lumbermen's and farmers' and miners' heavy boots to the daintiest shoes young women display and the little white kid boots for the baby's first steps. Black, tan, gunmetal and all the other colors of the shoe trade's spectrum were included.

The principal product was, and still is, men's and youths' everyday shoes, for which the wearers pay from three to four dollars a pair. No high-priced shoes. "Better shoes for less money," was George F.'s principle, and he advertised it to the world. Other manufacturers called Endicott Johnson and Company the Fords of the shoe business because they spread throughout the United States cheap shoes that looked good, felt good and lasted long. There is more profit in selling millions of shoes to the multitude than in selling mere thousands to the lovers of luxury.

While this progress was gratifying, it did not satisfy George F. Johnson. "The man who is satisfied is through," he often tells his people. He was not content, though the sale of Endicott Johnson shoes increased by twenty per cent in less than a year. As he reflected upon the greater volume of business that resulted from selling direct to retailers, he wondered whether there were not some other way hitherto untried which would add to the sales. Why not sell direct to the wearers of shoes through Endicott Johnson's own stores? This at first seemed the most logical thing to do.

But there was a catch in that—would not the regular retailers and the independents both quit selling E. J. shoes if the company opened stores in competition with them? Probably they would. It was necessary to make a careful survey, so as to be sure that E. J. stores should not interfere with E. J. dealers, and even then it was best to go slow. The company leased one store in Binghamton, another in Johnson City, and filled them both with complete stocks of shoes. These stores displayed the sign, "Endicott Johnson Community Shoe Store: Shoes For the Whole Family," and the company published big advertisements in the local newspapers, calling attention to the high quality and low prices of E. J. shoes.

The stores did a thriving business from the outset. People from towns fifteen or twenty miles away, in New York State and Pennsylvania, came there to buy shoes. Obviously the next thing to do was to open stores in those towns to supply the local demands. After these had prospered, the company began to spread the establishments farther and farther, until in the two states there were more than thirty E. J. retail stores, all doing well.

The retail business grew so fast that the company

built, in 1905, a large five-story sales and distributing house at Endicott, devoted to filling the orders of the retail trade alone. By 1914 an extension had to be added to this which doubled its size. The shoes in stock covered six acres of floor space, moving out almost as fast as they came in by truck from the Johnson City and Endicott factories. Meantime, in 1908, Endicott Johnson erected a similar distribution house on the west side of New York. On its side was blazoned their device, a widespread hide bearing the motto, "Endicott Johnson: Better Shoes For Less Money." This depot lessened the crowding of the house at Endicott by supplying the retail trade in New England, eastern and southern New York State, eastern Pennsylvania, New Jersey and Delaware, and it gave hourly service to New York City stores. As more stores were launched farther westward, they were supplied through these two depots.

By 1919 the Johnsons were convinced that their retail selling was not only profitable but an aid to their trade in all its branches. The same advertising helped them all, supplemented by displays in the local newspapers of the cities and towns in which they had stores. For these they supplied attractive reading matter and pictures of the latest creations in shoes that helped the sales. Still watching the field, to be sure of not hurting the business of established retailers, they steadily pushed their stores westward as far as Kansas City. The demand for E. J. shoes steadily increased, so that, in 1925, the company had to build a sales and distributing house in St. Louis. This was as large as the others, and the office force alone numbered two hundred twenty-five. From this warehouse the company supplies independent retailers in the western states and down to the southern end of the Mississippi valley.

The entry of chain stores into the shoe business brought a new demand for E. J. shoes. The chains do not manufacture shoes, but order their stock from the makers. Their orders are shipped direct from the E. J. factories in the Susquehanna valley, where they are handled through the Empire Specialty Footwear Company, a subsidiary concern organized by E. J. to take care of this class of business. Empire has offices in the city of New York, as well as in Endicott, to supply the department stores. The shoes are made in the styles and with any special features the chain store people may desire, and stamped with the brand of the store. The same methods are used in supplying the needs of mail order houses, which sell millions of pairs every year.

To sum up, the Endicott Johnson Corporation distributes one hundred seventy-five thousand pairs of shoes a day in the following ways: 1. Sells direct to the wearer through its own stores, of which there are now some four hundred in the country; 2. Sells through jobbers to the trade, as it did from the beginning; 3. Sells to the independent retailers through its own three large warehouses; 4. Sells to chain stores and department stores through the Empire Specialty Footwear Company; 5. Sells to the big mail order houses direct from the factories.

While the selling and distributing organization is directed by a vice president of the company and a sales manager, George F. and Charles F. Johnson, Jr. confer with them often, hearing and offering new ideas for selling shoes, while George W. centres his attention on the hide markets of the world and on providing the twenty-nine factories with an unfailing supply of leather. George F. still has the intimate knowledge of the E. J. shoes and the enthusiasm that inspired him, in 1901, to sell more of them than two pretty good salesmen could, and he pushes the sales today with the same zeal.

The squad of thirteen salesmen who went out in 1904 to call on the trade had increased, in 1934, to two hundred forty-five. They are on the road all the year round. Twice a year the men of the various divisions get together, at St. Louis, New York or Endicott, to compare experiences and tell how they have been able to increase sales. Those whose territory is too far off, gather in hotels and meet the chiefs from division headquarters. Sales resistance and how to overcome it is not much of a problem, for dealers and wearers know the comfort and durability of E. J. shoes.

Their chief object is to help their customers lay in

styles of shoes which will best appeal to the latest demands of the wearers. At the Endicott meeting George F. makes a brief address to the salesmen—not the ordinary "pep talk," but a few words about how good the shoes are and how everybody in the big family of workers is backing up the salesmen's efforts by doing his part well. And the same spirit is reiterated and stressed by the chiefs at all the meetings of the salesmen.

By maintaining production well in advance of distribution, the Endicott Johnson organization keeps their workers busy during the year, with very few idle days. They manage to avoid the long lay-offs and the feverish rush seasons that occur in other shoe factories. With their stock of raw hides and tanning materials always ready, they can turn out new styles of uppers and fancy leathers in any quantity at short notice, while there is always a reserve of sole and other staple leathers on hand for the ordinary demands of the trade. Long experience in business, aided by a sort of sixth sense that anticipates coming wants, enables them to escape seasonal lags in production.

"You keep the damn wheels turning, George F!" an old tanner shouted when the workers were congratulating Mr. Johnson, in 1931, on the fiftieth anniversary of his arrival in the valley. His son, his nephew and the other executives all help him to keep the wheels turning, not by guesswork but by a long look ahead. Together they go over the records of sales for the last year and note which lines have been sold in largest quantities.

How can these be improved so that consumers will call for still more? One after another suggests a change, perhaps very slight but enough to give the effect of novelty, which many customers seem to welcome. When they have agreed on what will most likely appeal to the fancy of the buyer, they show it to the chief stylist, and he, with the aid of one or two of his ten designers, produces the model. It may be modified several times before it goes into production. When it is put on the market the sales are watched, and if it meets favor it is made in large quantities. If not, it is dropped.

Endicott Johnson representatives attend the meetings of manufacturers, stylists and retailers twice a year at the Hotel Astor, New York. These men come from all parts of the country, and anyone who has noticed a trend toward a certain type of shoe tells of it. They all watch the college towns with keen eyes, for it is well known that what appeals to undergraduate boys and girls is apt to sell well throughout the country.

Besides, the Endicott Johnson style scouts—salesmen, artists, everyone with a keen eye for change—constantly watch the current drift of fashion. Anyone who discovers a novel idea reports it in detail to the Endicott Johnson stylist. He selects the best of these, modifies them to suit his ideas, and lays them before the executives. They pick out what looks most attractive and have a few thousand pairs made and distributed on trial. The customer who looks at the many styles offered him and says "I'll take these," little guesses the planning and labor that have joined to please his taste—nor how far his choice may go in influencing fashion for the time.

Advertising helps to attract people to E. J. shoes, and the company relies chiefly on the shoe trade journals, which reach jobbers and retailers. They make no extravagant claims, but they never fail to insist that they make "Better Shoes For Less Money." That slogan is repeated over and over again, though otherwise the advertisements are modest to the point of understatement. They are careful never to single out any particular type of shoe as best, for to do so might promote its sales to the disadvantage of other types. The company gives to retailers pictures of the latest novelties, in the shape of cuts which they include in their local advertising. Endicott Johnson spent $1,000,000 in advertising in national periodicals during 1928, but did not find it profitable enough to continue. They also spent more than $250,000 on a radio program three times a week, in 1929, but it drew little attention from customers, as proved by tests.

The officers and directors of the company and many others in the department of sales and distribution attended a banquet given in the Endicott Diner at the end of the campaign. The genial gentleman who had promoted it made a fine speech. He hurried past the failure to produce results by spending $250,-000 on radio, and told with fine eloquence of the marvelous results that were bound to flow from a new radio campaign, at a cost of a mere $265,000 more.

"What I'd like to know," said George F. when the orator stopped; "what I'd like to know is, where the hell we're going to get the mere $265,000?"

So the eloquent gentleman went back to New York, and the Endicott Johnson people went on with their trade journal and local paper advertising.

Besides the printed and pictured advertisements and the visits of the two hundred forty-five salesmen, Endicott Johnson has a more intimate contact with the retailers. They make more than a thousand kinds of leather shoes and, too, one hundred fifty types of rubber footwear, and among all these there flows a change of styles as constant as the change of the seasons. To enable the merchants to meet these changes, the company sends out to more than thirty thousand shoe stores, well in advance of the approaching season, letters, circulars and booklets which describe the coming styles, often in color.

Let us look at the circular about rubber footwear which Endicott Johnson distributed late in the summer of 1934, so that retailers could anticipate the next demands of their customers. Ordinarily one thinks of these goods as sandals, arctics and rubber boots—but they are merely the grand divisions of a multitude of devices to keep feet dry. In the circular mentioned, four large pages of calendared paper, with photographs reproduced in four colors, the company gives details of no fewer than seventy-one novelties about to be put on the market.

These range from women's black, all rubber, four-buckle, fleece-lined dress arctics to men's knee-high black blucher hunting pacs with red sole, and men's four-buckle, heavy work arctics, all rubber red sole. In between are such items as misses' storm rubbers; men's Alaska black rubbers, with British style toe or London style toe, to suit the wearer's fancy; women's brown or black front snap, cuffless, snap shoe with Cuban heel or spike heel; women's black, one-snap, all rubber gaiter, fleece-lined, with low heel; men's red, semi-storm rubbers, with white soles; the latest basket-ball shoe of white or brown duck and rubber, with a heavy leather insole, cool and long-wearing under the hardest usage.

But these are only the high spots in the circular. Every model described and pictured is typical of its class, and there are many varieties besides, to suit every taste. The company assures retailers who buy their goods that they will give satisfaction and insure a reasonable profit.

Also in the late summer of 1934, Endicott Johnson mailed to the retailers throughout the United States a large, twenty-four page book that fairly described three hundred forty-nine new styles of leather shoes, with two hundred ten rotogravure pictures of individual models, in four colors. Most of these were to retail at three dollars a pair or less, but there was a full page, with ten photographs, of Geo. F. Johnson shoes and oxfords, to retail at four dollars a pair. They were all low cut except one type of black kid bluchers, and chauffeurs' black calf bluchers, with rubber heels, full double oak sole and special insole arch support.

Every one of them had a smart, well turned out appearance, with graceful outlines and half a dozen styles of decoration in the toe-caps and on the tops. The next four pages showed an array of three dollar shoes, nearly all oxfords, called the Endwell style, with a bewildering variety of ornamentation, including the perforations and general streamlined effects then coming into popular taste.

There were pages of men's scout and service shoes, of men's and boys' nailed work and scout shoes, and boys' and ladies' high cut models for sport and field wear. A whole page was filled with boys' everyday oxfords, including moccasin bluchers in black and brown leather. Next to them came men's unlined welts, scouts and stitchdowns, in tan elk, golden elk, Eskimo calf and other tough leathers.

Ladies', misses', girls' and children's footgear oc-

cupied four pages, and extended from the most so-
phisticated patterns in various gay colors of fancy
leather, with slender heels of great height, to the
simplest designs of plain black or brown calf, with
broad soles and low heels, dear to emancipated
women. Perforated arabesquerie gave added attraction to many of them, wavy streamlines to others, and
there was a whole page of women's health shoes of
the most sensible models. Two pages were devoted
to little girls' and infants' shoes, broad of sole and
diversified with such ornaments as kiltie tongues,
gleaming buckles and gray lizard trim.

In the foreword of the book Endicott Johnson offer suggestions to the retailer which will help him
to make as lasting success in merchandising as they
have made in manufacturing and selling. Above all
else, the wearers of the shoes are the ones to be satisfied. Then they will come back for more, with a constant demand that insures steady profits. Many of
the difficulties that arise in the shoe business come
when the manufacturer, the wholesaler or the retailer forgets or ignores the consumer.

The aim of the company, as it has been from the
beginning, is to save every penny possible in shoemaking, from the raw hide and crude rubber to the
finished article—and divide the savings with those
who make and those who wear the shoes. Those who
stick to that principle are bound to prosper.

Many retailers, they add, will get a large share of

the business in their communities, regardless of the state of trade or the ability of their sales people, because they keep the consumer constantly in mind. He must buy new shoes as the old ones wear out, and he has not as much money as he had in better times. He shops around, finds that the Endicott Johnson product lives up to the claim, "better shoes for less money," and discovers a new way to get more for his dollar.

"Our entire proposition," says the company, "is based on this consumer attitude. The excellent values we offer will help the retailer to a profitable fall and winter business."

It is apparent that the E. J. spirit is active in its dealings with its customers quite as much as in its dealings with the workers.

"Every improvement we make," George F. Johnson has said again and again; "Every improvement and every saving we effect, is divided into three parts —the workers', the consumers' and the company's. That is one of the best ways to make a business successful and keep it so. People who sell our shoes and people who wear them know from experience that we give them at a low price the best leather and the most skillful workmanship. So long as we play fair with all three parties in the business, we can be reasonably hopeful of prosperity."

CHAPTER TWELVE

The Workers Talk to George F.

IN EARLIER chapters mention has been made
of the *E. J. Review* and its successor, the Workers'
Page in the Binghamton *Sun,* through which George
F. keeps in daily touch with his people. When the
business was small, he knew them all, and they freely
talked over their problems with him. But by 1919
the army of workers had grown to thirteen thousand, and such intimate contact was no longer possible. To keep the channel clear for open discussion
George F. began, on March 20, 1919, to publish the
E. J. Workers' Review, a monthly magazine, as the
place for questions and answers. It was really the
outgrowth of his instinct for neighborliness.

"If it is to be of any use in the world to either you
or the company," he wrote, "it must be a medium for
frank, candid and free discussion of our mutual problems and mutual relations. Don't waste time and
energy in complimenting the company or any of its
executives. Tell us what is wrong with this business.

Tell us what we can do to improve it. Show us how to improve it. Help us to do better. . . .

"There can be no permanent dislike or trouble among honest people who will get acquainted, who will compare notes with one another, who will talk over their troubles and their pleasures and their daily lives; who will take one another into their confidence, in order that they may make righteous decisions and righteous judgments with respect to one another."

Questions poured in. A childless worker, eight years on the job, wanted to know why the company gave preference to families with children in allotting houses. "I have heard much controversy upon the company's policy in this matter," he continued; "some of it pleasant and earnest; some of it scathing and unreasonable. One person said that from his point of view the object was 'plenty of shoemakers for the future.' "

Mr. Johnson replied that the houses were going to those who needed them most. "Greatest need," he added, "is generally present where there is a family of children, for the simple reason that landlords as a rule object to children. Hence those of us who have a family of children need these houses a great deal more than those of us who have a small family. 'The greatest good to the greatest number' has a very practical application in this policy. Do you not think so?

"After we have supplied the need at present so

great—selecting such as are most helpless and therefore subject to the greatest injustice from the methods
of the average landlord—we shall continue (I hope)
to build, and as many as desire may have houses. One
thing is certain: there will be no land values or
profits added to the selling prices.

"Much as the company needs factories and tanneries, and as full of possibilities of growth and development as the present situation is, everything must
wait now until these homes are provided. Until this
question is settled, the activities of this company will
be confined pretty largely to home building.

"Someone suggested that we were 'encouraging big
families and furnishing them comfortable homes in
order to secure future workers.' Right absolutely. No
camouflaging this question. But not right that we are
doing this selfishly; not right that we are exploiting
men and women for selfish purposes; not right that
we expect later to have these boys and girls in our
factories to do them any harm or to make their lives
less profitable and useful. That was the thought intended to be conveyed by the one who suggested this
as the reason why we encourage and try to help
large families.

"We hope to make this a splendid place for large
families. We expect, here in this valley, to make
Labor more noble—to dignify Labor with credit,
profit and honor. These 'born tanners and shoemakers' and those yet to be born, are born to a heritage—

The three Johnsons form a reception committee for a youthful delegation from Endicott's North Side

a heritage of happy, prosperous, comfortable existence, a chance in life to enjoy the blessings God intended that all should enjoy.

"If we build houses for big families, it is because
we see clearly a future generation of happy, well paid
workers, living under conditions as nearly ideal as
the state of civilization will permit at this age of
the world."

Another feature of the Endicott Johnson policy
which was not clearly understood at first was the
equal division of surplus profits between the workers
and the common stockholders, begun in 1919. Elsewhere such surplus goes only to stockholders—often
after deduction of generous bonuses to worthy chiefs
for their skillful management of the business. In the
Endicott Johnson organization the surplus was to be
split in half between certain stockholders and workers. No wonder such a revolutionary change puzzled
some of those who profited by it.

Early in 1919 the employees were invited to buy
stock in the corporation. At the same time the company made this announcement:

"Each year, after a seven per cent dividend has
been paid on Preferred stock and ten per cent set
apart on the Common stock, the balance of the
profits, if any, shall be split fifty-fifty between the
workers and the owners of the Common stock. Every
worker who has been in the employ of the company
throughout the whole year will share and share alike,

which means that the highest paid and lowest paid worker, and all between, receive the same amount, either in Common stock or cash, at the option of the directors; division made once a year. Plan commences as of January 1, 1919. First division made as soon as possible after January 1, 1920. . . .

"We have today the strongest and best leather and shoe business in the world. We shall continue to build and develop this business with your coöperation as rapidly as good, conservative business judgment permits. We congratulate the corporation that it has such a splendid organization of loyal workers. When we have good years, you will share them with us; when we have poor years, you will share the disappointment also. . . .

"This plan—the result of careful and conscientious consideration—is offered as our best conception of what Industry really means. Just as long as this plan works satisfactorily to all concerned, it is our intention to continue it."

This would seem fair to the average citizen. But one of the workers wrote to George F., asking this question:

"Your plants, I understand, were operated twenty-five years before you started the profit-sharing. Yet the workers, as earners, were entitled, under what you today call the Square Deal, to share in the profits of the past fifteen or twenty years, were they not?"

"No, they were not," was George F.'s answer, "because we had not arrived at the point where we considered, as an addition to wages, a profit-sharing plan. It is a comparatively new idea in industry. . . . The profit-sharing plan is a tardy recognition of the fact that the working partners must have greater consideration in the distribution of the general profits between Labor and Capital. Furthermore, our profits in the early stages were comparatively small and were needed to build new factories, new tanneries and to satisfy Capital. The possibility of profit-sharing never occurred to us until within two years ago, when I felt it was a proper thing to do and the thing we are coming to.

"Things which come to the lives of humans in the process of evolution are not necessarily retroactive. We all suffer more or less from injustice. We are generally satisfied when the remedy has been applied and justice becomes our portion. We are not, as a rule, prone to ask readjustment of past omissions.

"Profit-sharing is a mighty small beginning toward harmonizing the relations between Labor and Capital. Coming before it are other, more important things. It is, in fact, the last thing I could think of as a 'remedy.' "

Another worker wrote to George F. that he thought profit-sharing was a splendid thing, but—

"As an employee I would like to know why it is necessary to divide the profits equally between the common stockholders and the employees. If the common stockholders were all employees, I would say it is perfectly fair, but not as fair as dividing all the profits among the employees. I assume that many of the common stockholders are outsiders, whom you speak of as 'working not, neither do they toil.'

"I believe that the profits should go to those who create them, namely, the workers."

George F. replied that he thought the question was perfectly natural, showing an opinion generally held by the workers, and he would try to answer it fairly.

"First," he declared, "the worker has had a fair, liberal wage and good working conditions, with reasonable hours. Second, Capital has had very good interest on a fairly safe investment. Both, therefore, have been paid. In the operation of a business as fortunately situated as our own, a business where profits are made possible after Labor has been well paid and Capital has been well paid, because of original and economical methods of creating leather and shoes, there is likely to be a big surplus each year.

"As to whom these profits belong, there has been, and is, some difference of opinion. My view has been that they belong both to Labor and Capital, in equal proportion. Hence the profit-sharing plan. They certainly do not belong to Capital, although Capital has in the past assumed that this was true, and has taken to itself all the profits. They certainly do not all belong to Labor, although I assume that Labor would, if they could, take all—just as Capital always has—

A room in Your Home Library, Johnson City

A view of the Ideal Home Library, Endicott

until there is more in evidence a disposition to be fair in the operation of Industry. . . .

"My firm belief is that the company is disposing of that surplus in a fair and equitable manner, and that no reasonable person could find fault with this distribution of the surplus created by the joint efforts of both. The writer says that if the common stock-holders worked in the business he would not object to their having a share of the profit. He will therefore be glad to know that most of the common stock is owned by those who work in the business, by those who created the business, with the help of Labor."

Mr. Johnson pointed out that common stock-holders must wait for their return until labor had been paid and preferred stockholders got their seven per cent.

"Therefore," he continued, "all risk is taken by the common stockholders, meaning all the risk of loss, the risk of dull, bad years, the risk of rapid deprecia-tion and ultimate failure—if you admit there is such a risk: I don't. But there are bound to be bad years, and the common stock is therefore taking a risk. For that risk, they divide with the workers on the surplus, if there is any.

"Now this, to me, explains fully why the com-mon stockholders should share with the workers. It may not be as illuminating to all the workers. They may still have mental reservations and pertinent ques-tions. But to those who have these thoughts and questions, all I can say is that, with such knowledge as we had and such ability as we possessed, we have honestly tried to build up an industrial proposition on the Square Deal plan, and we feel that we have in a large measure succeeded. We believe the workers will agree with us."

Some workers felt that those who had been with the company for many years ought to have a larger share than the later comers—the old argument of the men in the parable who had borne the labor and heat of the day. Others complained that it was not fair to exclude able, faithful workers who had put in almost though not quite a full year on the job.

Mr. Johnson explained that in the new policy of sharing the surplus profits, all were starting from scratch, because the profit came from the efforts of all during one particular year; also that if eleven months, or even fifty-one weeks of work were entitled to share, this would work injustice to those who had put in the full term. There had to be a standard of service in making the distribution, and the company believed one year was the fairest standard to all. To make variations or exceptions would lead to confusion, to lessen the reward of those who had worked the full year.

The workers received, early in 1920, their share of the surplus for 1919, according to program— $237.90. The checks came out by the thousands, George F. receiving the same amount every worker in the business during that year received—instead of hundreds of thousands, or perhaps a million dollars, like some widely advertised corporation heads. Every employee—tanner, cutter, stitcher, laster, treer, finisher, packer, shipper, truckman, down to the yearling apprentices—got the same amount. There was no "big melon cutting," as was the fashion of the time. The good thing was evenly divided among all, the high, the middle and the low.

The biggest surplus checks up to 1934 were for $245.44 each, in 1925, when the average wage was $1,309.88 for the year. In this reckoning was included the pay of men and women, skilled and unskilled, of beginners, sixteen years old and upward—not of full grown men and women only, as the wage is sometimes averaged. And executives' salaries, which would have raised the average, were not reckoned.

Also to be included in this wage picture is the lower cost of living in the E. J. communities. This amounts to from twenty to thirty-five percent less than in other regions, thanks to the cheaper housing, the E. J. markets, recreational facilities and the medical care, for which the workers and their families pay no direct fee. Not charity—simply good management. All these things, carefully calculated, are paid for by adding two and one quarter cents to the cost of each pair of shoes the company sells.

Up to the end of 1930, the workers received some $15,000,000 as their share of the surplus profits.

After six and a half years of useful service, the *E. J. Workers' Review* was discontinued, in November, 1925. It had provided a forum for the free exchange of ideas. Most of the workers signed their letters, but some remained anonymous, because the writers disliked publicity. George F. understood why they shrank from print, and whenever an unsigned letter complained of anything that seemed unfair he investigated the matter and published the facts with his comments. For a time after stopping the *Review*, he issued a weekly letter, posted on the bulletin boards of all the shops. Finding this too one-sided, he decided after some months to hire a full page daily in the Binghamton *Sun*, in which the workers and he could discuss their affairs without fear or favor, and find all the news of the factories and of their friends. He has always acted on the belief that frank understanding of one another's views is vital to harmony throughout the organization. He believes that friends who trust one another and listen to both sides of any question are most likely to agree when all the facts are told and freely discussed. Five minutes of talk, face to face, will do more good than several letters; but as this is impossible with nineteen thousand workers, the next best thing is the daily forum on the Page for a prompt exchange of ideas. This keeps the air clear of misunderstanding, leaves no smoldering discontent that might impair efficiency.

A letter of complaint, even though anonymous, gets an immediate reply, and the two published together make interesting reading. One who signed his letter "A Friend" wrote, in September, 1934, to George F.: "You are now taking some of your own medicine. The government's going into the leather and shoe business in competition with you is just the same as your going into the practice of medicine in competition with those who are trying to get a living in the practice of medicine."

George F. replied in display type, four columns wide, at the top of the Page:

"There is some difference," he wrote, "unnoticed by our medical critic. We 'practice medicine' through the building of hospitals and purchase of the best and latest equipment to be used in medical work and research; through the employment of high-grade, skillful physicians, nurses and attendants. We place before our working people every known chance to recover lost health and prevent illness. We 'practice medicine' in fact, through a modern, co-operative plan. It does not put physicians out of employment.

"How, then, can our 'Friend,' writing that we are 'taking our own medicine' when the government seeks to enter the shoe and leather business, find logical reasons for his statement?

"Of all the good things we have found practical, the Medical Service is the best. Of all the bad things the government have found themselves able to do, going into business is the worst.

"Where is the Square Deal in the mind of our 'Friend' who makes the absurd statement noted above?"

Next day one who called himself an old time E. J. worker wrote from Endicott: "Yours is a leather and shoe business in which you have been very successful. Why not attend strictly to business and not reach out in a dozen little enterprises and deprive others of their business? You are in the restaurant business, bakery business, dance business, etc."

The writer complained that too many young workers wasted money on one-dollar dances at George F. Pavilion, and that it was not consistent for George F. to preach economy while he offered entertainment that cost too much—even though the Pavilion receipts were given to charity. George F. remarked that he published the letter so that the workers could see and understand some of the opposition the company had to meet.

Another E. J. worker, who signed his letter, wrote next day that "A Friend" was a mere "medical axegrinder," and added: "The E. J. Medical department is not only the finest, most practical and important gift our management has granted us, but is one of the most vitally important concessions granted by employers to a group of workers anywhere in the world."

Another worker wrote, over his signature, that by building homes and opening markets the E. J. company rescued the workers from profiteers. "Even during the depression," he added, "when many were afraid to build, E. J. kept building homes that gave work to many in different trades. In the nation to-day five million new homes are needed. If other firms would get the gumption and start to build like E. J., we would have work for contractors and carpenters for a long time to come."

One of the workers in the group that began to buy provisions in coöperation before George F. took hold and helped them to extend their buying so that all could share, wrote on the Page: "Endicott was suffering the characteristic evils which affect a booming town when its mushroom growth became public knowledge. Restaurants were charging exorbitant prices for 'Endicott chicken,' as hamburgers were called. Rents were far beyond the rents charged in many large cities, and groceries were rocketing until they reached the point where even our good wages of war-time were inadequate to cope with the greed of avaricious merchants." This worker signed his letter.

There was lively discussion among the workers in the fall of 1934, when some wanted to have George F. Pavilion turned into a gymnasium over the winter, and many wrote letters urging that this be done. The company leased a hall and an armory for gymnasium use four times a week, and asked the E. J. athletic association officers to get the opinions of their members. The Pavilion idea was dropped.

George F. wrote a letter to the Page, expressing satisfaction, and added: "All the gross receipts taken in at these dances are promptly paid over to the Broome County Humane Society for the relief of the suffering needy. When you attend the dances and enjoy yourselves so thoroughly, it will not embarrass you to know that the entire proceeds are given for relief, while the expenses are paid for from some other source of income. Let me emphasize—all the receipts, nothing deducted—last year's figures, $59,-962.98."

During his winter stay in Florida George F. is in daily communication with the Page. Workers' letters are forwarded to him promptly, and he answers them without delay. One might regard the Page as the nervous system of the Endicott Johnson organization, that keeps all parts of it in instant touch with one another and with the directing mind. It provides, as well as mere print can provide, the comradeship that began when George F. was at the bench and gathered around him the best crew of boot-treers in the business.

The Endicott Johnson Market at Endicott

CHAPTER THIRTEEN

The Worker at Home

DURING my stay in Endicott and Johnson City, in the summer of 1934, I was impressed by the way in which the company has made it possible, without paternalism, to provide for the workers' comfort and contentment in their homes. In the building operations, the legal services without fee, the markets open to all comers, the company restaurants, the home-making schools for workers' daughters, no less than the medical care and recreational facilities, the same friendly influence appears.

Endicott Johnson workers live in the country, with the conveniences of the city in their garden homes. These homes reflect the increase in the company's prosperity as well as George F.'s unceasing efforts to improve conditions. To go from the small houses near the old Pioneer Factory, cramped and crowded because the Lester company sold cheap land to workers at high prices, to the roomy homes at Endicott and West Endicott, sold at cost or less on the George F.

plan, is to follow the path of evolution from the old days of let well enough alone to this employer's belief that industry thrives best when all faithful workers are enabled to live well.

Because the Endicott Johnson company's business grew faster than they anticipated when they bought farms and created the manufacturing town of Endicott, in the early nineteen-hundreds, land sharks got hold of tracts near by and prevented a full development of the George F. idea. But in the village of West Endicott, near by, the company bought thirteen hundred fifty acres, in 1922, and at last were able to realize their ideal of a workers' community. In all three towns the visitor realizes that here people are living in comfort. They enjoy all the urban advantages, including churches, libraries and excellent public schools; with sunlight and fresh air unlimited; and with plenty of room for children to play and grow up into happy, normal human beings. The people have the self respect that comes from living in homes of their own.

Convenient to Johnson City, Endicott and West Endicott are broad fields belonging to the Endicott Johnson company. They are divided into garden plots, in which the workers cultivate vegetables in part of their leisure time. Many have gardens in the back yards of their homes; but some two thousand of them use the bigger plots in the fields, which are plowed, fertilized and harrowed free by the company. There they raise enough vegetables to supply their families during summer and fall, besides a generous amount of staples to put down for the winter. The men have fine farming exercise in the open, and they save money.

As you go through the streets of the three towns, see the people in the factories, in their homes, in the movie houses, the libraries and the recreation parks, see the girls and women shopping in the public markets and department stores, you are struck by the air of ease and good nature on all sides. Here and there you see a face with anxious eyes and wrinkled forehead, but these are very few. Strangers riding in the New York subway trains or struggling through the tides of humanity on the platforms comment more on the sadness of the faces than on the hideous crowding. In these towns it is just the opposite—the people are so alive, so cheerful. Another striking thing is that you see no loungers. Everyone seems to have some definite thing to do, and to be going about it briskly.

For several years I have had occasion to go through Lawrence, Lowell, Haverhill and other New England mill and shoe towns as the men and women came out of the shops at the end of the day's work. The contrast between them and the Endicott and Johnson City people was decided. Not that the New Englanders look sad or depressed. It was worse than that. Their faces were blank. They seemed apathetic, bored, like sleep-walkers—as if the monotony of their long day had worn out the capacity to feel joy or pain. As they moved on like automatons no one spoke or smiled. The only sound was of the shuffling of many feet, or an occasional click when two dinner-pails touched.

You do not see dinner-pails in Endicott Johnson towns, for they are as extinct as the dodo. Picnic baskets by the hundred, but no dinner-pails is the rule. That is because the workers eat their noon meal, freshly cooked, well balanced and appetizing, in the E. J. restaurants convenient to every factory, where they pay only fifteen cents apiece, though the cost is often more. To carry cold food in a dinner-pail would mean bigger expense and far less comfort.

In the Susquehanna valley the picnic is more than a habit; it is an institution. From May until autumn picnics by the hundred go out every afternoon. On Saturdays and on Sundays after church they run into the thousands. Sometimes two or three families make the excursion together; or thirty or more workers from the same floor join forces under the trees for a little feast on the grass, while their wives visit and the children play. There never was such a country for picnics.

With so many good picnic grounds available, it is not easy for the workers to choose. They may go to C. F. J. Park in Johnson City, or to En-Joie Park in Endicott, or to the high groves on Round Top at

Group of workers in native costumes

West Endicott, with a view for miles up and down the valley and a pleasant breeze sweeping up from the river. And by way of variety, parties often go up to the forests on the northern hilltops, two or three miles away—in their own cars, of course. Sometimes the outing is a clam-bake on the farm of a worker, a few miles out of town, where the men enjoy steamed clams, beer and baseball. Often George F. drops in for a visit; sometimes all four Johnsons are in the party—no formality, just four more workers with their friends.

Workers and their families find something of the picnic atmosphere in the Endicott Johnson restaurants outside of working hours. George F. established the lunch rooms to supply hot meals at midday instead of the "few chunks of boloney, slices of bread and a bottle of tea or coffee—all cold," which he and his fellows had to put up with for years. During the summer you will see on the Workers' Page every day an invitation to the E. J. families and their neighbors to come in any time after five o'clock for supper. The dishes are attractive and especially selected for hot weather, with generous supplies of cool drinks and ice cream. Many families come in at this time of year for the evening meal, which costs less than the materials would cost in the market. And the relief of escaping from the hot kitchen is something that only mothers with hungry husbands and children can appreciate.

Often the restaurants serve as social centres. The workers in one room get together for an evening dinner in honor of a friend's birthday, or a whole factory celebrates some event or an anniversary, or any one of scores of reasons will call a group to a feast. They have songs and dances and instrumental music by workers and their children, and a dance to follow until ten o'clock, with an orchestra of a dozen pieces. And you will often find George F., his brother C. Fred, and their sons among the guests of honor. Frequently their wives and children are with them. These dinners do much to strengthen a spirit of comradeship.

Workers have another friendly meeting place in the company's public markets. Bread at half the ordinary price is only the beginning of the economies the Johnsons have provided for the workers and the whole community. In the E. J. markets at Johnson City and Endicott, on Tuesdays, Thursdays and Saturdays, they buy every kind of first class food from twenty-five to thirty per cent cheaper than in town and city stores for miles around.

Farmers bring in fruit, vegetables, poultry, eggs, milk, butter and cream, veal, lamb and pork. Heavy meats, fresh and salted, are supplied at wholesale prices. Oranges and other citrus fruits are brought in carload lots from Florida. Selling direct to consumers, farmers get better prices than middlemen pay them for their stuff. Housewives do not have to pay the two or three profits that are piled on retailers' charges. These markets are not for the workers alone; anyone may buy, and the neighbors come from miles away for the bargains. There is profit for both sides. The market is a coöperative concern, as it has always been. It began in this way:

When the World War sent food prices sky-high, in 1917, John S. Patterson offered a rescue plan to the trustees of the village of Johnson City. As a caterer he had had considerable experience in buying, and he was sure he could induce farmers to come in and sell direct to the people. The board voted $1,000 for the expense of the experiment, and George F. Johnson paid his salary. On August 25th, he brought in thirty farmers, who parked their wagons in a vacant lot and quickly sold out their produce. George F. Johnson furnished the money to give every farmer a bonus of two dollars for each day he sold in the market. In six weeks there were twice as many farmers on hand. All sales were for cash, and the market flourished.

In November C. Fred Johnson invited the market into the Fire Prevention building, and in spring made room for the wagons in the street near by. Harry L. Johnson bought a plot in Corliss Avenue, in 1920, and built a market house, after George F. had sent the manager to get ideas in the public markets in New York, Rochester and Pennsylvania towns. The sales increased from eleven thousand loads of produce in 1919 to twenty thousand loads in 1923. George F. continued to give the two dollar bonus until 1926, when the market became self-supporting. Meantime the bonus had cost him more than $50,000, and many a farmer had paid off his mortgage or bought his first truck with his bonus. Of late years each farmer pays one dollar a day for his market stall.

As food prices went still higher, in 1919–20, the manager bought staple foods in carload lots, thus saving the community from the exactions of profiteers. He sold nine thousand dollars' worth of ham at twenty cents a pound, when the retail shops were charging thirty to thirty-five, and six thousand dollars' worth of sugar at fifteen and sixteen cents a pound when the stores were charging twenty-five cents and more. George F. Johnson and his brother, Harry L., worked for hours, weighing out the food and handing it to the customers.

Down at Endicott a dozen shoemakers had already begun to buy ham, bacon and canned goods in wholesale lots once a week and divide them for cash on delivery. They did so well at it that George F. paid a laster full wages while he gave all his time to the business. It soon grew too big for one man to handle; so Mr. Johnson donated land in the midst of the tanneries and factories, and asked the Johnson City manager and his staff to run a market there. The people of Endicott flocked to it, including the families of

George F. and his son, George W. By 1933 the traffic had grown so great that George F. rebuilt and decorated a company garage and fitted it up with stalls and a restaurant, run by farmers' wives. A few weeks before the opening the manager died. His daughter and her husband, Erwin Tiffany, took charge.

At six o'clock in the morning of the opening day, while the farmers were arranging their stuff in the stalls, Mrs. Tiffany, alone in the office, wept as she thought of her father's disappointment in not living to see his dream of the new market realized. There was a tap at the door, and George F. entered.

"This should be a happy day for you," he said, "and a sad day, too; so I thought I'd come around and say a word. This market is going to be a great help to all of us. Good luck. Good morning." He shook her hand and went away.

The public markets were not an unmixed blessing. The grocers and butchers of Johnson City, in 1920, wrote to George F. Johnson complaining that the public markets were ruining their retail trade. Mr. Johnson replied, saying, in effect, that he was encouraging the public markets to help both the farmers, who are the producers, and the consumers; employing the same methods so successful in their business, namely the elimination of unnecessary costs. Then he added: "The middleman is needed; he will always have a place in industry and in every community. But there need not be so many stores of all kinds."

Every year since the opening of the first market, George F. Johnson has been the host at a picnic to the farmers and their families at En-Joie Park. In welcoming them to the festivities, he often reminds them that they and their neighbors in the valley are helping themselves to happier lives by helping one another. At the 1933 picnic he told them he was planning to build a new market at Johnson City, for the old one had grown too small to serve all who came there. He sent the market manager and the architect to study the newest public markets throughout the country, and on their return, building was begun on a city block he gave near C.F.J. Park, in the centre of the town.

There was some delay in opening, because the company was obliged to borrow the building to store thousands of cartons of shoes when retailers quit buying because the Federal government seemed likely to begin making shoes. When that project was abandoned and the shoes were moved out, the market was opened in September, 1934, amid great rejoicing. Three hundred fifty farmers from Broome, Tioga, Delaware and Chemung counties brought their choicest produce, and George F. and Charles F. Johnson, Jr., and clergymen and civic officials made brief addresses.

The building is of steel and brick of light color,

eighty by two hundred feet, with a T-shaped addition, sixty by one hundred eighty feet, giving in all
forty thousand square feet of market space. There are
two hundred stalls, with five midways for trucks, a
washroom for vegetables, a flower division, departments for live and dressed poultry, rest rooms and
restaurant, all well lighted and air conditioned. It
cost $100,000, and grading and paving the surround-
ing concrete parking space for consumers' cars cost
$20,000 more, all given by George F. Johnson. On
one face of the building is a large stone tablet in-
scribed in big letters, "John S. Patterson Market,"
and on the other the motto offered by George F.,
"Live and Help Live."

An indication of the value of the markets may be
had by noting their steady growth. In 1919, the
farmers sold eleven thousand loads of produce for
$286,559; in 1923, twenty thousand loads for $647,-
776; in 1928, nineteen thousand loads for $833,943,
and in 1933 twenty-three thousand loads for $1,000,-
000. On the total sales during seventeen years, the
people of the E. J. communities have saved on their
purchases, at a conservative estimate, more than $1,-
250,000.

Another great saving for the workers is the legal
advice and service the company provides. Busiest of
law offices in Broome County are those to which the
E. J. workers resort. George F. Johnson established
the department in 1924. The workers pay no fee.

They pay nothing to their counsel, whose bills and expenses are met by the company—out of that two and one quarter cents added to the cost of every pair of shoes turned out in the factories.

The Johnson City office is devoted entirely to the needs of the workers, and its work has, of course, increased with the growth of the army of workers. For example, in January of 1929, this office held thirteen hundred fifty professional interviews. The total cost of legal services for that month was $13,-978, and the incidental expenses were $1,420, which saved $11,657 in legal charges to clients. At this rate the workers, coming to this office, would save more than $130,000 in legal expenses during 1929—and the amount of work done and money saved has doubled since that year.

The workers of Endicott, North Side and West Endicott go to the law department of the company in the Sales Building at Endicott. There the officers of the corporation and its employees are advised by the same attorneys, who give as careful consideration to one as to the other. It was not uncommon, in 1934, when certain parts of the N R A code regulations needed interpretation, involving thousands of dollars, to see one of the Endicott Johnson attorneys turn from analyzing a set of complicated rules to listen to a worker who needed help in taking care of his property, or wanted to make a will, or give bond in the Surrogate Court for his administration of a small estate. The amount of service rendered to workers in this office is about equal to that performed in Johnson City.

It is interesting to see how readily Europeans are assimilated in the Endicott Johnson family. Large colonies of workers of foreign birth live on the north side of Johnson City and Endicott. For a quarter of a century Italians, Poles, Russians and Czecho-Slovakians have lived side by side on terms of friendship and coöperation. The racial and national rivalries, which lead to jealousy and sometimes to bloodshed in many industrial communities in other parts of the country seem to be forgotten here. Whether this circumstance is due to the workers' greater intelligence, which breeds moderation, or whether it is the effect of the E. J. spirit, which they see in practice all around them every day, the result is the same —a community in which the various peoples respect themselves and respect one another. The foreign-born do all kinds of work, from manual labor to the most skillful operations in making and even in designing shoes. In the factories and in the schools their children show ambition and persistence that carry them far.

Throngs of children in the parks and playgrounds are the first characteristic a stranger notices in Endicott North Side. It is an attractive and tidy little city in itself, with a foreign atmosphere that is hard to define but which the visitor senses. The various nationalities have, as in many another community, flocked by themselves. The Italians are nearest to the factories, the others a little farther off, but all are united by community spirit and are proud of their homes. The older people keep up some of the old customs, but their children let them lapse. Some of the Italians have opened stores to sell groceries and delicacies from home; others have restaurants, with music and dancing. The Russians have their homes and two churches just north of them, the Russo-Byzantine architecture and spiral turrets lending an exotic note to the scene, their interiors enriched with sacred paintings in vivid colors. There are three Catholic churches and one Presbyterian on the North Side.

"I built my house here ten years ago," one of the Russian orthodox congregation remarked to me as we were walking out of the church one Sunday noon. "That is my house behind the four maple trees. I am a tanner since fifteen years; have always plenty work."

"What do you think of George F.?"

"Well," said the tanner slowly, as if weighing every word, "he is our friend. He gives good pay, but you must work for it. You see, he is doing for the people what the Soviets think they are going to do. He is all right."

Five experts from the Soviet shoe industry at Moscow, who spent a week in July, 1934, inspecting the

E.J. shops, told me they thought the workers there were better off than any others they had seen in this country, but they would not compare their condition with that of the Soviet workers.

The Russians have several social clubs, which often give entertainments, sometimes featuring three or four couples who wear the costumes of the old home and dance the old folk dances; but these are echoes of the past rather than part of the daily life. The younger element prefer modern American music and dancing. At the Epiphany season youths of Russian families used to make up with beards and ancient costumes, representing the Shepherds of the Nativity and the Three Wise Men. They sang from door to door and received little gifts, but the practice has waned.

Yet there are enough natives of the old world to keep alive many of the customs. Three thousand Russians, Hungarians and Czechs attended a picnic given on a Sunday afternoon in August, 1934, by the people of St. Michael's parish, at Stella-New Ireland Park, near Johnson City. Forty-eight girls and twelve boys, trained by native teachers, performed intricate Russian calisthenic drills and marches. On the next Sunday, the Sokol Slet, the general meeting of the Russian clubs of the valley, took place at the same park. Teams of young folks drilled and marched in competition, and the best performers won silver cups. The dancing that followed these events was American, with few folk dances that the older ones enjoyed. None of those present dressed in their native garb. Old world legends are taught to the children, but the actual practice of the old customs is dying out.

Most of the Czecho-Slovakians live in the eastern end of the North Side, though all three colonies overlap one another, and there is actually no segregation. This group has men's and women's societies that keep alive the old culture at lectures and dinners and balls, but the great majority of the folk seem as American as the people of Bangor or Augusta. In the whole summer of 1934 I saw only one woman at work in her garden with a shawl over her head and shoulders, European fashion.

There is no lack of churches on the North Side, and the Johnsons have helped them for years. Here is a typical instance:

One Friday afternoon in 1929 George F. Johnson halted his roadster near the new St. Joseph's Roman Catholic Church, on a North Side hill. A crowd of young Slovaks, Endicott Johnson workers, were helping their pastor, the Reverend Florian C. Billy, O.M.C., to complete the building, which had been held up by hard times. Father Billy was in overalls, driving a truck, and he went on with his grading work. At seven o'clock the next morning Mr. Johnson was there again, and when he saw them all hard at it, he smiled and got out of his car.

"I congratulate you," he said to Father Billy, "on

the way your people take hold of this work, of all their work. They never have 'laid down' on me. They have helped themselves, never hounded me to help. I love them for it, and here's what I'll do. Tell them I'll match, dollar for dollar, whatever money they raise to finish building this church." Within two weeks the congregation had pledged $28,000 for the work, and George F. gave his check for a like amount. Later he gave an organ.

St. Joseph's, of Gothic design, built of brown stone, is one of the largest churches in the valley, and all its interior decoration and its intricately carved woodwork have been done by the young men of the parish.

One of the finest buildings on the North Side, near the Hillside Centre Library, is the Temple of Duca degli Abruzzi Lodge, Order of the Sons of Italy. Its emblem is the Golden Lion, symbol of greatness and power. It has seven hundred members, pledged to take an active part in American life, to help one another, and "to maintain the love of our native land, and to cultivate respect for and gratitude to the land of our adoption." The women's branch of the Order, the Lodge of Princess Marie Jose de Savoia, was instituted in 1933, with a banquet attended by nearly a thousand members of the colony.

From time to time, members of the Order have presented plays in their native language at the Temple. But the language is studied by few, and year by year the old customs are disappearing. In former years the colony celebrated the feast of Our Lady of Mount Carmel with processions through streets gay with bunting and arches of electric lights. But since 1930 the processions have been abandoned, because the older folks do not feel up to parading, and the younger ones have outgrown the idea. The feast of San Marco has been for some years the occasion for a mammoth picnic at En-Joie Park, with a few old-fashioned Italian games mixed in a program of American track and field sports.

The visitor to the North Side, seeing these peoples of foreign birth living in harmony, in homes all neatly kept, contrasts the scene with the occasional racial clashes in other industrial centres. In all parts of the country colonies of immigrants are taught their duty by priests who speak their language, and the children receive regular instruction in the public schools. In Endicott and Johnson City and Binghamton they have worked and lived for years under another tranquillizing influence—the Endicott Johnson spirit in the tanneries, the factories and in the communities—the spirit of friendly coöperation.

It is significant of this fact that the foreign groups have elected the Johnsons honorary members of their societies. The idea was further expressed by a spokesman for the Sons of Italy, at a crowded meeting in 1933. He said: "Much has been written of George F. Johnson's material gifts to his fellow workers and the good he has accomplished in the community, but there is one thing he has given us that we must strive always to hold sacred—his philosophy of life." Dr. Jaroslav Novak, Consul General of Czecho-Slovakia, praised that philosophy and its effects when he conferred upon George F. Johnson, at a dinner at Binghamton, in 1928, the Officer's Cross of the Order of the White Lion, sent by President Masaryk. Six hundred Slovaks and other E.J. workers were present.

A similar gathering assembled in the Endicott High School about the same time, when Consul Pasquale Spirelli, representing King Victor Emanuel III of Italy, conferred upon George F. Johnson his appointment as Cavaliere of the Order of the Crown of Italy, an honor rarely granted to a foreigner, in recognition of his friendly help to Italians in his neighborhood. Justice John J. Freschi declared that Mr. Johnson is "a humane employer, a humanizing influence, a great Americanizing influence to any foreigner." In his speech of thanks Mr. Johnson paid tribute to the Italians as workers and as citizens. Smiling as he held up the rich insignia of the Order, he remarked, "This is going some for a shoemaker."

One of the most popular institutions in the valley is the school begun by Mrs. George F. Johnson, in 1917. Trying to find the best way to help workers' wives and daughters, she took counsel of a lady who had been for years principal of a school attended by many children of foreign parentage. She said: "I believe I'd begin with cooking. Mothers have told me again and again, 'Our husbands eat such good American dinners in the E.J. restaurants that they don't like old country dishes any more. If we could only learn to cook American!'"

That was the beginning of Ideal Training School, which has been ever since not only a powerful influence in Americanizing children of immigrants but has shown them and thousands of other American girls and women how to make homes healthier and happier. Twenty mothers came to the new school, in Ideal Park, and learned eagerly how "to cook American." More came from year to year, and many still come from the North Side where there is a smaller school, attended by mothers and their younger daughters.

Little girls enter Ideal school at nine or ten and begin a five-year course in home-making—not in domestic science with frills. Girls employed in the factories and about to be married sometimes come back for a post graduate course. There is no tuition fee. Mrs. Johnson provides the instruction and the materials free. In the first year the pupils learn plain sewing and darning, how to use the gas stove and cook simple meals. They sweep and scrub, make beds, learn how to keep a house neat and clean. As they advance, they go to market with their teachers and get practical experience in buying foods.

A clam-bake group, with George IV. and Charles F., Jr. present

Charles F., Jr., C. Fred, George F., and George W. with a group of workers at a clam-bake

Often a class of girls cook and serve a dinner for their parents at the school. They learn, too, how to wash and iron clothes, how to buy the materials and make their own dresses and keep them at their best. There are evening classes for those who are busy during the day. In the school there is a suite of rooms— hall, living room, bedroom, kitchen and dining room, in which the girls practice everything from furnishing and decorating to preparing and serving attractive, wholesome meals. Saturday mornings in 1933 there were three hundred sixty-nine girls in the morning sewing classes and four hundred eighty in the afternoons, most of them from the E.J. factories. One afternoon they made forty dresses for themselves, besides other work. In the classes in 1934 there were over seven hundred children and two hundred sixty-seven mothers and employed girls. Not all of them finish the five years' course, but eighty received certificates for having completed all the terms. Each girl cut, fitted and sewed her graduation gown.

The libraries of the valley play an important part in the cultural life of the workers and their neighbors. Ideal Home Library in Endicott and Your Home Library in Johnson City are community centres as well as libraries, supported by the citizens, housed and largely aided by the Johnsons. They are liberally stocked with books, magazines and newspapers; they are the homes of clubs, societies and schools of citizenship. Their activities are so diverse that librarians come from other regions to study their methods, especially in guiding children's work and play.

Organized by the people of Endicott, Ideal Home was chartered in 1916, began with a thousand members in a rented store, and soon had to hire more space, to accommodate a club room and kitchen. Thirty thousand volumes were taken out in the first year, and story hours for children were so popular that still more room was needed. Children were reading fifteen hundred books a month. The library was supported by subscriptions, with State and village aid, until 1917, when the company took the responsibility for its finances. The village board still appropriated $500 a year for its support.

One of the souvenirs, which the staff shows with pride, is a letter from George F. to the librarian at this time:

"Certainly. Get any books you want, now and always, and send the bill to me. I count the expense mighty little compared to the benefits which are so abundant when one sees the boys and girls and the older ones enjoying the use of the Home and the books."

There was already a colony of foreign-born workers on the North Side before Endicott Johnson began to build workers' homes there. Children from the North Side flocked to the Ideal Home, but few of their parents came; therefore the E.J. service department fitted a motor truck with shelves, which the librarians filled with books, in English, Italian, Slovak, Polish, Greek and French, to interest the parents. It was one of the first traveling libraries in the State. Four thousand volumes were borrowed in the first summer by foreigners eager to learn American ways, and librarians gave them friendly counsel on their problems of citizenship.

Mr. and Mrs. George F. Johnson, finding that the service of the library had increased five-fold, bought a large, handsome residence on the block next to their home, in 1918, and gave it to Ideal Home. The number of books was doubled; there were four new clubrooms and a large assembly room; often as many as two hundred fifty children gathered for the story hour; there were rooms for cooking and sewing classes; members took out sixty thousand books during the year, and the staff was increased to fourteen. The company built and equipped the Hillside Centre library, in 1920, as the North Side branch of Ideal Home, and spent $15,000 a year to support the two. At Hillside Centre they established a babies' clinic, play school, organized games, and classes in sewing and canning.

Mrs. George W. Johnson organized cooking classes at Hillside, in 1924, and they have attracted more mothers and daughters every year. They receive the same instruction as the pupils in the Ideal course, and their training is of great value in making them familiar not only with home-making but with American manners and customs. Every month from one hundred fifty to one hundred eighty mothers and daughters are busily engaged three times a week in learning to be American as well as "to cook American." They are divided into small groups so as to get the most intimate attention from the teachers. Twenty girls were graduated in 1932 from the full five-year course. There is no rigid, formal program of Americanization. The girls acquire American ideas easily and naturally as they advance in their work. Some of them asked for a class in American etiquette, and studied with interest the difference between the social conventions of the old world and the new.

So many other interests had come into Endicott in 1925 that the company asked the village trustees to take charge of the library, meantime continuing their contributions. The two institutions had, in 1934, more than twenty thousand volumes, including seven hundred in Italian, Slovak, Russian and Greek, at Hillside Centre. They take regularly more than one hundred magazines, periodicals and newspapers, and there are seven thousand ninety-nine registered borrowers on their lists. Their motto is, "As many books and as much help as possible for the greatest number of people at the least possible cost."

Your Home Library is a large mansion on Main

Part of the crowd of twenty-five thousand persons enjoying a circus performance at En-Joie Park, during the 1934 May Day celebration

Street, Johnson City, which George F. Johnson bought, equipped and gave to the people in 1924. It is managed by the village trustees, on an appropriation of $10,500 a year, and the company contributes whatever else is needed, usually $5,000. Your Home is the centre of most of the social activities of the village, and it includes besides the library and reading rooms, a dining room, children's room, mothers' room, sun room, smoking room and rooms for dancing and supper parties, with complete installation of gas ranges, kitchen and table ware. Here, as at Endicott, social and literary clubs, the Red Cross have their headquarters. Mr. and Mrs. Charles F. Johnson refurnished and redecorated the building in 1934.

The library had eighteen thousand books in 1934, an increase of two thousand during the year. One-third of the one hundred fifty thousand books borrowed were histories, biographies and scientific works, which is a pretty good proportion of non-fiction for any community. Nine hundred fifty-four children attended sixteen story-hour meetings. Two hundred sixty groups of about twelve thousand persons used the club room in 1934.

Mrs. Charles F. Johnson, Jr. has maintained and directed a sewing school at Your Home since 1925. Here girls from ten to fifteen years are taught every kind of needlework, from plain stitching and darning to the finest sewing, by hand and on machines. They learn how to cut and fit their clothes, and the thirty girls out of two hundred ninety who finished the course in 1934 wore dresses of their own design and making. Mrs. Johnson gives a Christmas party every year—since 1919—to twelve hundred or fifteen hundred children at the High School, with a tree and Santa Claus, and a present for each one, all provided out of the gross receipts of the George F. Pavilion. Mrs. Johnson also devotes much time to the students in the Nurses' Training School at Wilson Memorial Hospital in Johnson City. After graduation exercises every year she gives a party in their honor in the beautiful gardens of her home.

One carries away from the valley the picture of a busy, vigorous united community of people, who work hard, play a great deal, and enjoy life to the full. The homes, the schools, libraries and churches, and the parks present a scene that lasts long in memory. One visitor remembers an August evening in 1934 that was typical of the place and the people. In a worker's garden we dined under an arbor, on a steak broiled over a camp grill set on the lawn. Not far away the trees of George F.'s home were in sight, and looming above the northern prospect was the huge bulk of a group of factories. Here, indeed, was the worker truly at home.

CHAPTER FOURTEEN

Medical Service and Health Promotion

THE Endicott Johnson Corporation guards the health and well being of its people. Its department of Medical Service ranges from advising expectant mothers and caring for all workers' injuries or ailments to easing the last days of the aged, and providing for the wants of bereaved families. Its doctors also serve the E. J. Workers' Sick Relief Association, an independent, voluntary enterprise, which provides cash for its members.

None of this is done in the way of charity, which any self respecting citizen resents. The medical department is supported by a coöperative plan through which the workers and the company both contribute their share of the cost, which is greatly reduced by paying for it wholesale. Everyone who has been six months in the organization may take his share of the Medical Service when needed. Enjoys it as a right, not as a favor.

The efficiency of the army of nineteen thousand

workers, whose health and comfort are kept at the maximum, compared with their efficiency if left to haphazard treatment at the last moment, is something hard to estimate. The difference goes beyond any mathematical calculation. But that is not all the gain. It counts in the morale. One can imagine the worker's sense of security when he knows that every possible safeguard is provided for his health—and, if he should fall ill, he has neither doctor, nurse nor hospital to pay. He knows that all he needs to do is to get well as soon as possible.

And the best part of the whole business is that the staff of thirty-four doctors, four dentists, twenty-six graduate nurses and their sixty helpers devote their skill more to keeping people well than to taking care of the sick. Starting with one doctor and a nurse to take care of people injured at work, the system has grown gradually into a means of general health promotion.

All share alike in the enterprise. The owners, the executives, the workers and their families, are treated by the same doctors and with the same facilities. If anyone feels run down, not up to his best, he consults the company doctor and follows his advice. Whether he has a trivial ailment quickly set right, or needs an operation that keeps him in the hospital for weeks, he knows he is as welcome as the president of the company or any other official.

"When our Medical Service was new," the head

of a department told me, "I took my wife to Albany for an operation, which cost more than four hundred dollars, and then found out that our own surgeons would have done it quite as well—without any fee or hospital bill to pay. And I discovered that the Johnsons and all the other chiefs rely on our own Medical Service when they are sick. I learned my lesson right there, and ever since we and the children have gone to the Medical, too. There is none better. I thought I was in for appendicitis last spring; but our doctors gave me a thorough examination—X-rays and everything—put me to bed in the Johnson City hospital and kept me on a special diet for three weeks. I came out as good as new."

Though the medical department is now one of the most important parts of the E. J. organization, it has grown from a small beginning. As confidence in it increased, the company added to its scope. Something slightly resembling it was attempted as far back as 1896, when the Lestershire company, from its Boston office, invited its employees to join a Mutual Benefit Association. Each worker was to pay dues of ten cents a week, and to this sum the company proposed to add a total of three dollars a week. Sick or disabled members were to receive five dollars a week for not more than eight weeks.

"It is earnestly to be hoped," the distant owners wrote, "that all the employees of this Company who are eligible will join this Association, and thus do away with the constant passing of subscription papers and annoyance of giving occasionally where same is not deserved." But the Lestershire owners' earnest hope withered. The workers were not drawn to their rather chilly proposition, and nothing was done.

The Endicott Johnson company, which hitherto had not studied this particular problem, offered, in 1916, a more attractive plan. They proposed a Sick Relief Association, to which each worker was to pay twenty-five cents a week—if he thought it worth while. The company was to contribute weekly a sum equal to what all the workers paid. There was no urging. "Membership is entirely voluntary and does not affect a person's standing with the company in any way," was the invitation. A member was to receive twelve dollars a week during ten weeks of sickness. The directors of the association were to be made up of one worker elected by the members in each factory. Six thousand out of the ten thousand workers, including most of the executives, joined the Sick Relief Association. The rest were willing to take their chances, but as the plan showed good results more came in. In 1934 thirteen thousand out of the nineteen thousand E. J. workers were members.

The Medical Service is a separate organization. Under the Workmen's Compensation Law, superseding the old law that relieved employers from liability if an injury to a worker could be laid to "carelessness of a fellow servant," employers were obliged to provide medical aid in case of industrial accidents. The law did not require that a doctor should be in constant attendance in a factory, but in order to avoid delay George W. Johnson, in 1917, engaged a doctor and a nurse and fitted up a small infirmary in the Sole Leather Tannery at Endicott. By treating slight injuries at once, they reduced infections to a minimum.

With machinery protected by safety devices, there was no great demand for medical service in accident cases but often workers came in to be treated for headaches, indigestion and other ailments. Sometimes a worker, laid up at home, felt that he could not afford to call in a doctor, and thereby lost a week or more through illness which could have been cured quickly with prompt treatment.

George F. watched the experiment with deep interest. Seeing how much suffering and time were saved by the doctor and nurse at the tannery, he engaged another doctor and nurse, and had all four visit workers sick at home—if they so desired. The workers did not take to the innovation at first; but the medical staff became members of the E. J. organization, made their homes in Endicott, and gave the workers all their time. They began to be popular.

After watching the experiment for a year and talking with workers who had been treated by the doctors, George F. could see that taking care of what seemed to be trivial ailments prevented serious illness and loss of time from work. He increased the Endi-

cott staff and urged his brother, Harry, in charge at
Johnson City, to engage more doctors there.

"The chief trouble, George," said Harry, "is to
find the old fashioned kind of doctor, who is willing
to go into the homes of the humble. We can get
plenty of modern physicians, who like to practice
in fine homes, but the other kind isn't so easy to find."

It was no longer difficult to find doctors when many
came home from service in the World War and began to look for practice. Before the end of 1920, six
doctors and as many nurses were serving the workers
of Endicott, and four doctors and four nurses were
busy at Johnson City. Superintendents of factories
found that fewer workers were absent because of
sickness, and that they came back to work sooner
after being ill. Men steadily at work were more effective in the constant effort to make better shoes for
less money—and the increase of comfort in the community meant a better morale in the shops.

As the workers found themselves better off under
the care of Endicott Johnson doctors, their confidence in the service increased. Many who could afford private physicians preferred to call on the doctors they knew as neighbors. George F. was convinced
that medical care was not only making his people
happier but was increasing efficiency, and he de-
termined to provide enough of it.

"We are going to be able to take care of the great
bulk of trouble caused by illness in the families of

Sunday evening band concert at En-Joie Park

our people," he wrote in the *Review*, "but we must have a little time. We expect to improve rapidly from now on, and render fuller and better service to all."

As we have seen, it was almost by accident that the company discovered the value of providing medical care. Having found it they added to it as a natural development of their desire "to extend our resources in all ways whereby the workers can be benefited." It proved to be wise business administration, but it was not begun as the result of a planned policy. It sprang from the friendliness which from the beginning inspired George F.'s dealings with his people.

In the *Review* George F. wrote to the workers, urging them to call upon the company's doctors, as he and all his family did; to use the Medical Service, which made it possible for them to be cared for without paying a fee. This encouraged many who had long put off seeing the doctor when they felt sick, because they thought they could not afford it. Sometimes examination would reveal that the worker was suffering from illness of long standing, which should be cared for in hospital.

With so many new patients, it became necessary to provide more hospital accommodations, so that all the sick could be promptly treated with the best methods. Mr. Johnson had subscribed liberally to the Binghamton City Hospital and the Wilson Memorial

Hospital at Johnson City, in 1919, and arranged to meet the expenses of his people there; but these were miles away from the Endicott and West Endicott neighborhoods, with thousands of workers and their families. Statistics quoted in the New York State Journal of Medicine, in September, 1924, declared that one American out of ten needs occasional hospital care. Even if the proportion were less in these industrial communities, the need was still there.

To satisfy this want, the Johnsons began a campaign of hospital building. They looked for sites with as much care as the sites for new factories— with even more care; for guarding the health of the community was so much more important. George F. and his brother, C. Fred Johnson, consulted doctors and architects to make sure that the new buildings should stand in pleasant, quiet places, with profusion of sunlight and fresh air and equipped with the best scientific aids to restoring health. They asked for suggestions from their sons and other workers. It looked as if they were going in to build up human vitality on the same big scale as they made shoes to sell.

What happened in the planning and building of Ideal Hospital illustrates the spirit in which the work was carried on through all the region. George F. Johnson, early in 1925, told the trustees of the village of Endicott that the E. J. company would give ground for a hospital near the water works, and

he would give $100,000 toward building it if the
citizens would appropriate an additional sum of
$150,000. They promptly voted a bond issue of $150,-
000, to be paid off in ten years. After further surveys,
the experts found that Round Hill, near Riverside
Drive, commanding a fine view up the Susquehanna,
would be a better site. George F. gave the land there,
and increased his money gift to $150,000.

A local architect, advised by Endicott Johnson
doctors and other local physicians, planned the institution. Local firms built it, put in the heating, light-
ing, plumbing and furnishing. Two years were
needed to finish the job, and then Ideal was adjudged
one of the best hospitals between New York and
Buffalo. It is a fine four-story edifice, framed of
steel, its walls of tile, covered with pale yellow brick
and stone trim. A sun porch of eighteen thousand
square feet, framed in glass, is a prominent feature.
Eighteen of the beds are available for private patients. Everything a modern hospital needs has been
provided, from examination rooms to the maternity
ward and nursery, biological laboratory and major
and minor operating rooms. Best of all, the hospital,
perched on a sunny hilltop, has a cheery atmosphere
that does almost as much good as medicine.

The hospital is governed by a board of trustees.
Any citizen is welcome to use it; any doctor may
attend his patients there, whether he is a member of
the staff or not. The fees are less than half of those in

large city hospitals. The Endicott Johnson company pays all charges for their workers out of the fund already described, but takes no part in the management. The total cost of the hospital was $338,000, the additional $38,000 being made up by gifts from societies and individuals.

When the hospital was opened, thirty-four beds were enough, but soon there was a demand for more. Seventy beds were added when the nurses gave up their quarters on the third floor, in the second year. They moved into the home built next door by Mrs. George F. Johnson in memory of her sister, Mrs. Anna McGlone Farrington, who died of influenza while serving as a nurse in the World War. It is a structure of steel, brick and Indiana limestone, in architectural harmony with the hospital, and it cost $125,000. Every nurse has her room and bath; there is an auditorium, furnished as a living room, which has a stage and can also be used as a ballroom. In the basement is a large drawing room available for community meetings.

Other hospitals in the company's system are the E. J. Workers' Hospitals in Binghamton, Johnson City and Endicott. Besides, the Johnsons have given largely to the extension and improvement of the Johnson City General Hospital, formerly the Wilson Memorial. Near this is the nurses' home, given by C. Fred Johnson in memory of his wife, Mrs. Ida F. Johnson. It stands on a hillside, three stories high at the front and four at the rear, a handsome structure of steel and brick, and cost $200,000. It contains eighty-five rooms and baths for nurses, each with an outside window, besides a large living and assembly room, suites for matron and housekeeper, doctors' offices, lecture rooms.

Long before this, in 1920, Mrs. George F. Johnson had given $100,000 to the Binghamton Hospital, to be used for any purpose the Board of Managers thought necessary. They built a nurses' dormitory, and she spent $20,000 more in furnishing it. Later Mrs. Johnson gave $40,000 to enlarge the maternity ward of the hospital. This provided for the addition of one more story to the building and an increase in the number of beds from twenty-three to sixty.

A doctor who made a survey of the Endicott Johnson Medical Service in 1924 and described its activities in a medical journal, reported that neighboring physicians commended it. He also declared that this "experiment in paternalistic medicine is probably the most extensive in the United States."

As a matter of fact, the service is not paternalistic in any degree. Money spent on it and all the other E. J. benefits is paid out of a fund raised by taxing every pair of shoes two and one-quarter cents. This amount is accounted for as part of manufacturing cost. That is, on every pair of shoes, so much is charged for raw materials, so much for labor, so much for management, so much for obsolescence of machinery, so much for taxes and a score of other items—and two and one-quarter cents for promotion of health and comfort.

When the plan was new, in 1919, a worker wrote to George F.: "Why don't you put the money to pay for these things into our envelopes? Isn't it our money? Are we not taxed to pay for these things? If so, wouldn't it be better for us to be permitted to select our own service and pay for it with our own money?"

George F.'s reply, published in the *Review* in May, 1919, was:

"If it were true that it is your money—yes. You should have it and do as you please with it. But it is not true.

"The total cost of all moneys used for recreation, for medical attention, for maintenance of restaurants above what we take in, for Sick Relief above what workers pay, for accident compensation above what the State allows, and for every kind of expense occasioned by our well known and well established policy with respect to these matters, amounts to two and one-quarter cents on each pair of manufactured shoes. This two and one-quarter cents is added to the costs of the shoes when they are figured. Therefore, it is not taken either from your wages or from profits.

"Doesn't the ultimate consumer pay for these things—inasmuch as it is added to shoe costs? We answer—no. It is conceded that this company furnishes better shoes at lower prices than are procurable elsewhere. We argue—and challenge contradiction—that we save this two and one-quarter cents a pair through increased efficiency because of these things, which make men and women feel like working and work more cheerfully and happily, and hence more efficiently.

"The theory of maintaining these things is based upon plain common sense. In combination, thirteen thousand people have better medical attention at lower cost. The doctor is at your service, no matter how slight the indisposition. You thereby prevent serious illness. You have prevention rather than disease.

"We desire you to know all about your business. We very much desire you to try to make it better and more profitable, and we want you to share fairly in everything you have helped to create."

At the time of this writing, 1934, the E. J. Medical Service takes care of nineteen thousand workers and their families, or sixty-six thousand five hundred in all, from Binghamton to Owego. The staff is made up of thirty-four doctors, twenty-six graduate nurses, four dentists, five dental hygienists, five pharmacists, three bacteriologists, and two laboratory technicians, four physiotherapists, one radiographer, four ambulances, twenty-one clerks and twelve other helpers. During 1933 the staff doctors made one hundred fifteen thousand house and hospital calls; visiting nurses more than eleven thousand calls. Besides, there were one hundred fifty-nine thousand office visits and twenty-nine thousand five hundred dental visits during the year, as well as outside doctors called in consultation.

An E. J. worker or his family can have medical attention at any hour of the day or night.

Industrial accidents are cared for by the medical staff. The company is self-insured under the law, and keeps $250,000 on deposit with the State of New York to meet all claims due. Injuries to workers are kept down to the minimum by practical instruction in all hazards and by careful installation of safety devices on machines. The total number of accident cases treated in 1933 was three thousand two hundred sixty-five, of which four hundred forty-seven were serious enough to receive compensation to the amount of $65,937.

There are able specialists on the staff. The major surgical work is done by the chief surgeon and his three assistants, who operate daily. In 1933 five hundred sixty-three major operations were performed. Diseases of the ear, nose and throat are treated by trained specialists. The removal of infected tonsils, so important in preserving health, is done by experts. There were fifteen hundred of these operations in 1933. Three laboratories, one in each principal hospital, are maintained, to assist the staff in chemical diagnosis; and the X-ray is used both for the detection and cure of many troubles.

Every worker seeking employment undergoes a thorough physical examination. If he has no serious defect, he is kept at work six months. Then, after passing another thorough examination, he is eligible to membership in the Sick Relief Association which, as noted before, is quite separate from the E. J. Medical Service. There is no compulsion to join, but thirteen thousand workers are members. Each pays twenty-five cents a week, for which he receives twelve dollars a week in case of sickness that keeps him from work more than one week and up to twelve weeks. In 1933 the workers paid premiums amounting to $159,091, and received $145,047.85.

Since the Association was formed, in 1916, benefits amounting to $2,793,129 have been paid, toward which the workers contributed only $1,900,322. Though it is well known that if a worker is in hard luck the company will not let him suffer, it is significant that more than two-thirds of the workers prefer to insure their own income when idle through sickness. They value their self-respect and pay their good money to protect it. This seems to be an effective answer to the theorists who say that if an employer helps his workers they will quit helping themselves and throw the whole burden on him.

When a worker or any member of his family is sick, the people of the Medical Service take care of

the case promptly. A treer at the Fine Welt Factory
stopped at the Endicott clinic early one morning in
July, 1934, and reported that his wife could not eat
breakfast and suffered so much pain that she had to
go back to bed. An ambulance was sent for her at
once. Within half an hour the treer was called from
his work to the hospital, where the doctor told him
she had appendicitis and should be operated on at
once. She was willing. Two hours later he was back
at the bench; and when he went home that evening
he found supper waiting for him. The Medical had
sent a capable, friendly woman to take care of his
children and keep the house in order. When his wife
came home, after three weeks in the hospital, the
woman remained. She stayed two weeks longer, to
make sure that the patient should rest and get her
strength back. All this service was paid for by the
company, out of the two and a quarter cents shoe cost.

The director of a room in the Scout Factory at
Johnson City noticed, early in 1934, that one of his
best men was falling behind in his work. He had a
constant little nagging cough and was growing thin.
The director persuaded Tony to drop in at the clinic
and ask the doctor to give him something for the
cough. Using the X-ray, the doctor found that Tony
had incipient tuberculosis, and told him he must go
to the mountains and get well. But what would become of his wife and two children—he wanted to
know. E. J. would take care of them, the doctor said,

and Mrs. Tony would receive his full pay every week. So he went up to the Adirondacks and lived in one of the two large cottages the company maintains at Saranac Lake. He found fifty-five other E. J. workers there. When he came home, early in the fall, he had picked up twenty pounds and was well; but his superintendent put him on light work out of doors, to keep him well.

Out at Kattellville, a few miles north of Johnson City, the company owns a large old house, done over in modern style, with a garden and a farm. Here women workers go for rest and relaxation when their directors notice that they are below par. They stay until their health is restored, living out of doors amid beautiful surroundings, with nothing to do but rest and stroll and get well. And if they have dependents at home, they know the company is taking care of them.

It is in the care of mothers and babies that the Endicott Johnson doctors excel. More than a thousand babies were born in the maternity wards of the E. J. hospitals, in 1933, and for months before their birth their mothers had received advice and treatment from a staff well informed in the best methods of prenatal care. Every expectant mother in the E. J. world knows that she will have the benefit of kindly and scientific attention from the moment she asks for it until she and her baby go home, in excellent health and fortified with the results of expert medical skill and good nursing. There are maternity wards in all the hospitals, and special clinics for babies and children in all three communities. There the doctors teach mothers how to keep their children well.

As I went here and there in the valley, I often saw groups of mothers and children sitting in the reception rooms of the clinics, waiting to consult the specialists who devote all their energies to this branch of medicine. Most of the ailments seemed trivial—colds, or a touch of indigestion, an aching tooth, or perhaps adenoids; but any one of them might develop into a serious condition unless relieved by the care of the doctors. It was the old idea of the ounce of prevention at work. The value of this preventive work has been proved in thousands of cases recorded in histories of welfare work for children. Mothers are informed of these facts at club meetings in the libraries, and they are quick to appreciate their usefulness. They have known from girlhood of the full scope of the medical service, and after marriage they call at the clinics many times before the day of greatest need.

Whenever it is needed, day or night, an ambulance calls to take the expectant mother to the hospital. One of the first things she sees after the birth of her child is a bunch of roses or a sheaf of whatever flowers are in season, from Mrs. George F. Johnson, with a letter of congratulations and best wishes and a check for ten dollars for the baby. Before 1933 Mrs.

Johnson's gift was a new ten-dollar gold piece in a red morocco case. The mother finds another present waiting—a little white box, in which is a pair of tiny white kid shoes for the baby and a card with the inscription, "Good luck to you all. George F. Johnson." Next day comes another gift from George F., a bank book which shows that ten dollars has been deposited in the Endicott Savings Bank to the credit of the infant. Until the mother comes home a woman from the Medical Service keeps house for her, and stays a few weeks longer, until it is certain that she can manage without help.

Mothers are invited to bring their babies to the nearest clinic every few weeks, so that they can be weighed and looked over, and changes of diet advised if needed to keep the child growing right. The many thousands of babies born in the E. J. hospitals have had the benefit of these clinics. Anything needed to insure the normal development of children is suggested there, and if they show symptoms of impaired vitality, they receive prompt treatment. Orthodontic work, to straighten irregular teeth, which ordinarily costs hundreds of dollars, if not thousands, is done at the E. J. dental clinics without fee.

Although the Endicott Johnson employees who suffer accidents while at work are insured under the compensation law, the company's aid to disabled workers does not end with merely obeying the law. The injured man is promptly attended by an E. J.

doctor, and if necessary a trained nurse is sent to his home to take care of him. Or he may stay in hospital. But, even with his compensation insurance, the worker may have more obligations than that sum will enable him to pay. He may have several small children, taxes and interest to meet, or sickness in the family. In all such cases the injured man's director tells the head of the Medical Service, who then calls on him, finds out exactly what he needs to keep going, and sees that he gets it promptly.

There is nothing formal or mechanical in the giving. There is no questionnaire to fill out, nor any prying into the worker's private affairs. If he has been employed by the company for years, one may be sure that he is a faithful worker, coöperating in the united effort that makes success, and in time of distress he is not forgotten. The Service officer knows this, and he drops in and discusses the situation with the sick man like an old neighbor. Together they go over the things that have to be paid, the resources on hand, and how much more is necessary. It is a friendly talk, not an inquisition.

If later the injured man can pay back all or any of the cash advanced, well and good; if he can't, that is all right, too. Simple as it might appear to be to take advantage of such generosity, it practically never happens that this is done. The relief staff have been on their job for years, living in the community and knowing their neighbors well; and they keep "the heart warm, the head cool" that George F. recommends. Often it happens that he or some member of his family takes a hand in the proceedings. In fact, it is hard to distinguish where the company relief ends and the personal relief begins. I heard of one case that is typical of many others:

At the time of the World War, when the company was trying to make shoes enough to supply the constantly increasing demand, a group of workers in the yard of a Johnson City factory, resting after the midday meal, were talking about strength. Dan Sargent —not his name, but near enough—a short, stocky man of middle age, with the shoulders of a wrestler, dared the rest to lift a can of shoe dressing that weighed close to five hundred pounds. They could not budge it. Dan took hold and raised one end of it a little, but could not get it all off the ground. The others laughed, and Dan tugged harder than ever. He struggled until his eyes bulged under the strain, and then the rest of the men made him stop.

Dan went home sick that afternoon, and his director reported to the Medical Service. The doctor found that his eyes were badly strained, and took him to the hospital, where in spite of the best efforts of the staff and the help of specialists who were called in, poor Dan lost his sight. If he had hurt himself while at work, he could have recovered compensation under the law; but the accident had happened at the noon hour, not when Dan was at work but was engaged in a sporting contest of strength. Under the law, he was not entitled to one penny.

But the Endicott Johnson company, after its representative had carefully looked up the facts, sent Dan his pay envelope every week. He had several growing children, and he needed the money—and that was that. George F. Johnson, who had worked close to Dan in the old Lestershire days, dropped in once in a while for a visit with his old companion.

In the slump after the war, when employment lagged because there was little demand for goods, and when the prices of all commodities had increased tremendously, Dan Sargent felt the pinch. It was very much on his mind when Mr. Johnson drove up one afternoon and joined Dan, who sat sunning himself on the porch of his house.

"How are you, George F.?" said Dan, as they shook hands. "'Tis great to hear your voice again. How are all the family?"

"All well, thank you, Dan," said the chief. "And how is it with all you folks?"

"In the best of health, thank God," said Dan. "But you know, George F., these times are something awful. We go on living through force of habit."

"Yes, times are bad," said Mr. Johnson, "but we've lived through worse, and we'll live through this."

"True for you," said Dan. "But I've had a heavy load on my mind lately. The price of food and clothes, the price of everything, has gone up so high in the last few months that we've been pressed very hard. It's that bad, I think I ought to have a raise in my wages. What do you think, George?"

"Well, to tell you the truth, Dan," said Mr. Johnson, "I haven't been thinking of it at all. But I see your point. Tell you what I'll do—I'll speak to the payroll folks about it and see what they can do."

"No fear but they'll do right, with yourself jogging them," said Dan gaily. "Well, I'm easier now with that off my mind."

There could be no doubt that honest Dan believed the gift he had been receiving every week for three years was not a gift at all, but wages. And when the boss was an old friend, why shouldn't he ask for a raise in wages when times were hard? And, just to show that Dan's reasoning was not all askew, the payroll folks did increase his allowance by more than half after Mr. Johnson spoke to them, and gave him the increased "wages" as long as he lived.

When time has worn down a worker so that he can no longer turn out as many shoes as in his best days, he is not thrown out on the scrap heap. He has no fear that slowing hands and dimming sight will banish him from his job. He knows that so long as he will do his best by the company they will do their best by him. Long before age slackens his pace, any falling off in his work is noticed, and generally the cause is found and removed. So that when time itself reduces his energy, he knows that an easier job will be found for him. Meanwhile his production record is constantly supervised, and any falling off starts an inquiry.

"What seems to be holding you back, Louis?" a director asked Louis Nietsch, a cutter in the Scout Factory. "Have you been under the weather?" Louis, an athlete, twenty-eight years old laughed at the idea of being under the weather. "Never had a sick day in my life," he said.

"You're behind your figures for last year," the director continued. "Do you think you'd like to try something else?"

"No," says Louis slowly, as he reflects. "I wonder if this could be it? I have had a headache nearly every afternoon lately—and, say, I've been batting .165 and missing a lot of flies out in the field on our ball team. Errors piling up against me. What do you know about that?"

"That looks as if your eyes might be bothering you," says the boss. "You remember Jimmy Waldron last year—how getting a pair of glasses stopped his headaches and helped him earn a lot more? Why don't you stop in at the clinic on your way home this afternoon, and let them look you over?"

Which Louis did. After a careful physical examination, which showed that his general health was first class, the doctor took him to the oculist. His tests revealed that Nietsch's right eye was fifteen per cent stronger than his left—astigmatism—and that his efforts to use the eyes together had made the condition worse and brought on the headaches. He prescribed glasses to correct the vision, and in a short time Nietsch was earning as much as ever—and his fielding errors were greatly cut down, too.

If it were not for such careful watchfulness, just as likely as not, the worker would not have found out for years the cause of his trouble, and he would have endured a great deal of discomfort as well as loss of earning power. Hundreds of E. J. workers have been helped in this way.

Easier work for slower hands is the rule. There are hundreds of odd jobs around the factories and in the yards, and they are all filled by old-timers, who do not earn as much as they used to but are glad to be at regular work, free from the horror of idleness. I was surprised to find so many old-timers among the workers still going strong at the bench. Hundreds of them have organized a Thirty-Year Club, who dine together twice a year and talk over old times with their friend, George F. They are still active in the company's employ, except for the women who have married.

But in the factories one will find many to whom thirty years at the bench is a record long surpassed. In the old Pioneer, for example, I met two treers who had been steadily at work there since George F.'s time, in the 1890's. One of them, tall and without a thread of white in his thick black hair, would pass

for fifty at the oldest. He is seventy. He wears glasses,
but he handles his job like a lad. The other, red-
haired and jovial, is a first-class treer. There seems to
be something in the E. J. system that attracts good
men and keeps them young. In the Johnson City
factories—oldest of the group—there are a great
many gray heads, lively survivors of early days.
George F. was seventy-seven years old in 1934, and
his brother, C. Fred, eighty—both of them hard at
work from seven o'clock every morning.

The Endicott Johnson employee who is too old to
go on working does not hesitate to say so and ask for
help if he needs it. He has not been paying in so much
a week out of his wages toward a pension fund or
retiring allowance. The money needed is included in
the two and a quarter cents figured in the cost of each
pair of E. J. shoes and previously mentioned. There
is no fixed, arbitrary pension, to be dealt out to all
alike. If a worker needs nothing, he gets nothing. If
he has a little home, without the means to keep it up,
the company gives him enough every week to take
care of it and of himself. If his family are in strait-
ened circumstances, he gets enough to insure their
welfare, too. If their condition improves so that less
help is needed, then less is given.

There is no fixed time or rule about retiring. Suppose a worker has been failing for years, with rheu-
matism or some other ailment gradually weakening
him, he simply tells his director at last that he can't

The swimming pool in C.F.J. Park, Johnson City

go on. The director notifies the head of the Medical Service—for this is another one of the duties of that organization. The chief of the Service calls on the worker, sees how he is situated, and together they figure out the sum he ought to receive every week in order to keep him in comfort. No questionnaire, no graphs, no sliding rule—nothing but good faith on both sides.

It is significant of the thrift of the great mass of the Endicott Johnson workers that at the time of this writing—1934—with ten millions unemployed in this country and millions drawing public and private relief, only fifty-nine men and women are receiving this help from the company. Fifty-nine out of nineteen thousand. The rest of the retired ones—many hundreds of them—live in their homes, supported by their savings, perhaps with some help from their children.

Twice in the months I spent in the valley I had the pleasure of looking at groups of these veterans. A more cheerful gathering you could not ask to see. They were not only cheerful but you could see they had preserved their self-respect. True, they were receiving help, but they felt they were entitled to it, had worked for it and now were glad to get it from their old boss, to whose prosperity they had contributed all they could.

In the great May Day parade in honor of Mr. Johnson in 1934, two busses at the head of the procession were filled with retired E. J. workers, who cheered George F. as they went past the reviewing stand. He waved to them with his warmest smile and watched them out of sight; for every man and woman there was an old friend, who had worked beside him in the early days of the Lestershire factory.

Many of these old-timers were being supported by allowances from the company; the others were living on their savings. But as they came into view, all smiling and waving to their old chief, you could not distinguish the pensioners from those of independent means.

"Are all these veterans on the company's payroll?" I asked an executive beside me.

"No," he said; "probably not half of them. Our people have the right kind of pride. They won't ask for help unless they actually need it. And if anyone asked for it when he was really able to take care of himself, he wouldn't get very far."

In the hour of death Endicott Johnson stand by their people. They have no formal scheme of life insurance for employees, with the payment of a fixed sum of money to the bereaved family as the end of their relationship. Instead they try to do what kindly relatives or intimate friends would do for them: maintain the protection of the home and provide a comfortable living for the widow until the children are old enough to take care of her and themselves.

What happened when Thaddeus Pollack died in

1933 offers a good illustration of the system. Pollack was for years one of the steadiest truckmen in the company's employ. As he was walking across the railroad track near Johnson City, a train struck him, inflicting injuries from which he died a few days later in the hospital. A trained nurse from the Medical Service took care of his wife, kept the house and prepared the meals for the five children. The company provided for the funeral and paid all the charges. Pollack had been putting most of his earnings into his home, and two of the children had been ill recently; so he left very little money.

The head of the Service called on the widow soon after the funeral, and found that she had no funds. On his report, the company sent to Mary Pollack every week the same amount her husband had been drawing as wages. She felt secure; she no longer dreaded that she would be compelled to put her little ones in an asylum while she went out to work.

Driving past the house with the head of the Service a few weeks later, I was admiring the neatness of the place.

"That family is a credit to our community," he said. "Pollack was one of our best men, and it was not his fault that he left so little. His widow is receiving his full wages every week, and will receive them as long as she needs them. The oldest boy will be sixteen next year, graduated from high school and ready to go to work.

"When he begins to earn, we may find that the widow does not need quite so much help every week, but there will be no change in the envelope until we have gone over all the facts with her and we are sure that she and the rest of the children won't suffer any deprivation. As the others grow old enough to work, the payments will gradually lessen, and stop when there is no longer any need—say four or five years from now."

Forty-eight widows and eighty children were supported by the company in 1934 under this plan. The highest number recorded was seventy-seven widows and three hundred twenty children, in 1927. Since the system was inaugurated, in 1919, the company has been taking care of at least forty or fifty fatherless families every year. It would be difficult to estimate how much better citizens these children will be, having grown up under their mothers' care, to say nothing of their joy in leading normal, happy lives.

George F.'s instinct to give for the joy of giving animates the highly individualistic beginnings which have evolved into the practical and successful E. J. system. It is reflected in the contribution of more than $170,000 which his employees have made to the relief organizations of Broome County since 1930. That instinct appears, too, in his large gifts to the hospitals of the region, to the Humane society, to all the churches in his neighborhood, and to the unfortunates in prison and the almshouse. It was at work in 1920, when he told his old chum to get a first class car and send the bill to him, and it has continued since. Every other year he reminds his friend to trade in the old car and send him the bill for the difference. It is not only his gift that counts, but the way he follows up the giving with continued interest and solicitude.

Year after year, as long as they lived, he delighted to visit the old companions who worked and played ball with him in New England, and swap stories of the hard knocks and good times they had experienced together. When he found his old shopmate and short-stop, Mike Fahey, tending a railroad crossing, he set the postmaster of Binghamton—his fellow visitor—to watch the gate while he and Mike went home for a visit. It was a joy to George F. to make Mike's last days happy and to spend $30,000 a year thereafter to ease the hardships of many other old chums.

His giving has been the very opposite to that of the pompous passenger who handed down a nickel to him to help pay his fare to Worcester when he was a boy—the only man who ever gave him money. It is evidence not only of George F.'s heritage from his mother but of the example she set when she was always giving to her neighbors and spending watchful nights with them when they were sick.

The tremendous success of the Company's medical and health promotion work becomes even more significant when it is considered in relation to the practise in American industry generally. There can be no question that George F. Johnson has gone further than any other industrialist in this important field. While a great many industrial concerns in the United States provide medical and surgical service for their workers, very few do so to the extent of the Endicott Johnson plan. Large corporations, particularly railroads and mining companies, which have a high accident rate, and those which operate in isolated districts, have their own doctors and hospitals. Manufacturers, with rare exceptions, are content to furnish surgical care for workers injured in their employ, as required by law, but in general do not concern themselves with medical service for ailments outside of that. One of the largest coal and iron companies maintains seventeen dispensaries and emergency hospitals in its widely scattered works and villages, with forty-six doctors and ninety-five nurses. The company pays for their services in accident cases, but in all others the workers pay their share of the costs.

In practically every instance, as with the Endicott Johnson company, manufacturers began to engage doctors when the workmen's compensation law went into effect, in 1917. Some of them have gone beyond that, but, whether the service is to sick employees in their homes or to members of their families, it is paid for in large part by the employees who use it. Four hundred forty-three manufacturing companies that responded to a questionnaire from the National Industrial Conference Board in 1931, reported that they provided limited medical care for their workers. Twelve of these concerns were listed as manufacturers of leather and its products, none separately as shoe manufacturers.

The two principal obstacles to the general adoption of the Endicott Johnson medical plan are, first, the widespread suspicion among workers that such service is furnished as a substitute for higher wages; and, second, the confident belief of most employers that they pay their people so well that they can afford to engage their own doctors. It seems evident there is not enough of the mutual good faith that comes from long and friendly association.

Diligent search has discovered very few employers who by their acts recognize the value of a healthy, contented community of workers as a big factor in efficiency, and fewer still who simply charge the expense of all social betterment as a legitimate part of the cost of their product, as we have seen in the E. J. system. The spirit of friendly coöperation which inspires the Endicott Johnson plan is generally lacking. That spirit is born of instinct, not calculation. Its results are beyond calculation.

CHAPTER FIFTEEN

Athletics and Recreation

Ten thousand workers, more than half the force in 1935, are active members of the Endicott Johnson Athletic Association. Four or five times a week, all the year around, most of them take part in sports promoted by the company. The great majority play simply for fun and exercise, but they have highly developed teams in baseball, basketball, track, golf, boxing and softball. The Eastern Branch, of Johnson City, and the Western Branch, at Endicott, struggle for supremacy with a rivalry as keen as you will find among the colleges or the professional leagues.

When the leading nines of the two branches, at the end of each season, meet in their local World Series for the championship of the Association, thousands of men and women cheer them on. And at all the big events and many of the lesser ones, you will find George F. and his family applauding the plays and enjoying the fun. At a tanners' clambake or picnic, George W. pitches a few innings now and then with a great deal of his old-time skill. Charles F., Jr. shoots a respectable game of golf, in the low eighties, and you will find him in team matches with his fellow-workers on holidays.

Baseball, the old national game George F. has played since childhood, is the sport out of which all these others have grown. There was no thought of the later development when he began, in 1904, to provide ball grounds for the workers as well as playgrounds for their children. He remembered the fun he and his fellow shoemakers used to have playing in the back lots and how it braced them up for hard work, and he knew it would be a fine thing for the E. J. workers, too. Therefore he contrived that new factories and new diamonds grew side by side

His love of the game prompted George F., in 1913, to buy the Binghamton professional team and bring them up from the cellar to the championship of the New York-Pennsylvania league. But after two years he wearied of being identified wherever he went as the owner of the champions rather than as the head of a great industry; so he sold the franchise and devoted his baseball talents to spreading the game among his own people.

George F. is as keen for the best in ball playing as in the making of shoes, and every year since 1905 he has taken a party of friends to the national World Series. His early years of strenuous play and his continued zest for sports have helped to preserve the energy with which, long past his seventieth birthday, he is able to direct his great corporation. Nothing strengthens the bonds of fellowship more than mutual devotion to a game, and fellowship is the keystone of the Endicott Johnson arch.

For an hour before play begins in a local World Series, a stream of workers, in cars and on foot, flows through Washington Street, Endicott, to En-Joie Park. Spectators pay a dime apiece to see a contest as thrilling as a big league game. Children go in free. The more ardent fans leave the shady grand stand and fill the rows of benches close to the back-stop screen and along the base lines among them sits George F., close to home plate, smoking a cigar and talking with a treer as he watches every move of the players. Two of them have refused jobs on professional teams because they would rather enjoy life at steady work in E. J. shops, and the rest are about as good. The wife of an Upper Leather tanner sits on a front bench, and divides her attention between his fielding and their two little boys playing with a toy automobile at her feet.

Wild yells of "Safe!" greet a Jigger batsman who slides to second base, but as he jumps up out of a cloud of dust the umpire thrusts down his left hand to signify he's out.

"I thought he was safe," says George F. to a ruddy-cheeked E. J. worker beside him who used to play

on the champion Binghamton Crickets in the eight-
een-eighties.

"No," says the old boy; "Joe caught the ball while
Jim was a foot away."

"Guess I'll have to take your word for it," George
F. replies, "but I thought Jim beat the throw by a
split second. Anyway, the ump was right there." He
offers a cigar to his neighbor, and they talk about
some of the great games the Crickets won fifty years
ago.

Scattered among the thirty-six green acres of the
park, half a dozen games of softball are going on,
contests among uniformed teams of men not young
enough for the fast game, some of them in the late
forties. One team is made up of directors and superintendents of factories, but on the diamond they do
not get—or expect—more consideration than anyone
else. These games last only five innings, because
longer contests take too much out of the players, and
fun is not allowed to interfere with efficiency. Even
the youngsters play no more than seven innings as a
rule.

Though the softballers know that the struggle at
the west end of the park is for the pennant, they
ignore it in the heat of their own battle. On the cinder track that circles all the diamonds a group of
mile runners are jogging, in preparation for the next
meet, but they barely glance at the big game, no matter how loudly the crowd cheers. Four young fel-

lows are practicing pole-vaulting not far from the
pennant contenders, but the game might as well be
in China for all the notice they give it as they hurl
themselves over the high bar, drop in the sand pit,
and go back to the runway. One is prepared to believe
that the habit of concentration in their work carries
over into their sports.

A burst of cheering in the sixth inning announces
that the Jiggers have scored their third run, and are
even with the Upper Leather Tanners. They have
been trailing, two runs behind, until now, and their
rooters are so tense that they forget to stand up and
stretch in the seventh.

"What's happened to Tom?" George F. asked,
when an Upper Leather batsman poled out a home
run, with men sprinting in ahead of him from second
and third, and the unlucky pitcher was taken out.

"Too much prosperity," said the old-timer beside
him. "He made ten bucks pitching a semi-pro game
Saturday, and today he has no control left."

With vindictive smashes the Upper Leather fellows tally twice in the seventh, but their third man
is cut off at second. Score: 5—5. The crowd hardly
dares to breathe. Now three Jiggers fan out in quick
succession, and Upper Leather comes to bat. The
first man up beats out a throw-in from deep left field,
and dashes across the plate with the winning run.
Slowly the crowd drifts away, groups still arguing

over close decisions that had started cheers and booing again and again.

"Pretty good game," the old Cricket short-stop remarks to George F., as they move along together toward the gate. "These boys got speed to burn."

"They're good," George F. agrees. "Of course, they have gloves and masks and pads to protect them, so they don't split fingers and lose teeth as we used to; "but they have the old fashioned team-work and fighting spirit. That's what counts, out there or in our business."

"That's right," says the old player. "Well, good day," and he strolls away as George F. responds, "Good day to you."

By hard work and perhaps a few lucky breaks, the Upper Leather Tanners' nine won the series from the Jigger Factory nine of Johnson City in 1934, three games to two, and brought the championship to Endicott for the first time in five years. Seven hundred admirers celebrated the victory with a banquet, in which the families of the players joined, in the great hall of the E. J. Diner at Endicott. The Johnsons, with their wives and children, were there in full force.

Each member of the Upper Leather team received a prize of twenty-five dollars, and each of the Jigger Factory lads received fifteen dollars. All the members of the other ten teams in the E. J. League received ten dollars apiece, including groundkeepers, scorers, umpires and photographers. These awards, some $2,000 in all, were the gifts of George F., his annual contribution to the game. In congratulating the winners, he reminded them that their competitors were almost as good as they were, and he praised them all for their hard fighting and good sportsmanship.

At the end of each outdoor sports season the Messrs. Johnson entertain the players of all the softball teams—East Branch, West Branch, boys, girls, bench men, superintendents and directors—at four banquets in the E. J. Diners at Johnson City and Endicott. These feasts are special occasions, to honor the ballplayers, but they are only a small part of the long series that the workers enjoy through the whole year, the Johnsons usually among them.

Some of the most interesting games played on the E. J. fields are the contests among the girls' teams from all the factories at softball. Of course, the girls are the pick of the athletic talent in the shops, but even though you know that before you go on the field, you will be surprised at their grace and stamina. Many of them are not long out of high school, where athletics is as much a part of the course as mathematics. They pitch underhand, as soft ball rules require, but they field and throw and run like boys. They wear smart uniforms—with shorts and sleeveless shirts. It is surprising to see these young women step up to the plate and wallop the ball with all the ardor of college boys. And how they can run! Their games, limited to five innings every other day, do them a world of good.

Sports have become so important a part of the Endicott Johnson program that they are managed by three workers who have withdrawn from their jobs in the factories to devote all their time to this activity. The company pays them all through the year salaries equal to what they earned at the bench. George F. Johnson had very poor places to play in as a boy, and now he is evening the score by providing sports for his workers by the thousand, on grounds given by him, his family and the company.

For many years I have studied the value of sane athletics as an aid to efficiency in all kinds of work, physical as well as mental, and have written much on the subject. There is no doubt that participation in sports refreshes a worker and enables him to do more than the man or woman who neglects the physical machine. Overdoing, of course, is as dangerous as over-eating or any other kind of intemperance. But a reasonable amount of lively play, with the added stimulus of competition, is a great asset.

That is the principle that governs the Endicott Johnson athletic promotion. Their baseball players, young athletes who keep themselves in prime condition, play only seven innings in a game, except the two teams in the final championship series, who play the regulation nine. The basketball players have a schedule that does not wear them out. Most of the boxers spar only for fun and exercise, and those who appear in public exhibitions box only three rounds of two minutes each, under the rules of the Amateur Athletic Union. The softball players play only five innings in each game.

I have come to the conclusion, after watching the various contests over a period of three months, that the Endicott Johnson Athletic Association not only furnishes healthy exercise for the workers but affords entertainment that makes them happier and enables them to do more and better work.

Although the workers had played ball and many other games for years, there was no formal organization of the athletes until the slack times of 1929 gave them more leisure. Then they got together in the Endicott Johnson Athletic Association, with forty-seven hundred members in the East Branch, which includes Binghamton and Johnson City, and nearly five thousand members in the West Branch—the workers of Endicott, West Endicott and Owego. All the year around the teams of these branches compete in many kinds of sports scheduled by the three managers, after consultation with the team captains.

Baseball leads the list. There are thirty-five teams in the East Branch, made up of five hundred twenty-five players, divided into a league of six hardball teams and twenty-nine in softball. The latter are: seven North Side, seven South Side, nine of superin-

George W. Johnson pitches the first ball in one of the opening games of the 1934 baseball season, Endicott Johnson Athletic Association

Charles F., Jr. tests his batting eye

tendents and directors, six in the Girls' League. The West Branch has more than four hundred players, four teams in the regulation game; the rest in softball, as follows: a league of fourteen teams of men from the bench, six teams of directors and superintendents, four nines of girls and women, and a league of eight teams in Owego. All of these play under strict rules. There is no drafting of a star performer from one shop team to another by a captain eager for a pennant. You play for your own factory, or you do not play in competition.

Softball seems to be the answer to the long quest by recreation experts for a game which combines the most fun with the best form of exercise, together with the least chance of injury. The bat is smaller than the regulation bat, and the ball is larger and soft as an orange. Like lawn tennis, which began as a gentle pastime, so softball was at first a very mild form of sport. A man could step into the field at any time and give a good account of himself, though he might be a little stiff in the arms and legs next day.

But under the stress of competition the game began to develop speed. Pitchers, though limited to underhand delivery like the primitive pitchers of regular ball, learned how to shoot the ball over the plate with twists that baffle the batter with his little stick. Fielders mastered the art of freezing on to the squirming, soft ball and putting the enemy out.

I watched many of these games, and found them as

full of surprises and thrills as the orthodox contests. And every little while the ball would wriggle out of clutching fingers or hop off at a crazy angle when it hit the turf and set everybody whooping. Everybody, that is, but the poor devil who failed to field it. When you mean business in any game, the sense of humor dries up and blows away in the heat of battle. What is a joke to the crowd is a tragedy to the player who is unlucky enough to let in a winning run for the enemy.

I noticed that the sixth and seventh innings of these games were played at a much slower pace than the first five. Men of forty and upward feel just as full of pep as the boys and try as hard, but their untrained hearts tire, and an hour of hitting, running and jumping to field the high ones wears them down. That means slower work next day and more likelihood of making mistakes.

The one point that doctors and physical culture experts stress above all others with middle-aged athletes is that, no matter how interesting the game may be, they must stop short of fatigue. But how can a game player quit? He'd rather drop in his tracks. The three athletic managers solved the problem by cutting down the softball games from seven innings to five. That made it easier for everybody, made the games refreshing instead of exhausting, a real aid to efficiency.

Wherever one sees the E. J. workers, in the factories or on the playing fields, they show the good effects of their sports. They are well set up, bright-eyed, alert, ready for action. Their most popular games are baseball, softball, swimming, basketball, bowling, boxing, golf, football, handball, pitching quoits, running, from sprints to the mile; jumping, skating, on ice and on rollers; tennis, tug-of-war, and volley ball. Ten thousand play, and one-fifth of them compete in sports—one thousand in baseball, indoors and out; five hundred at golf, two hundred at basketball, one hundred each in boxing and track and field events.

Each branch has a boxing master, a first class ring man, who teaches the workers his art. Some of them win glory at the public bouts held every few weeks, under the rules of the Amateur Athletic Union. Thousands of the workers and their families gather at the ringside to see the fun. If a contestant is out-classed, the referee stops the bout. Members of the E. J. Athletic Association pay twenty-five cents a year dues, and are charged only twenty-five cents a seat at the boxing shows, for which outsiders pay forty cents—about one-fourth of the price charged at similar bouts in the clubs. Members pay ten dollars a year at En-Joie Health Golf Club, outsiders a little more.

George F. Johnson has been a boxing enthusiast ever since he used to put on the gloves in his youth. I sat near him at the ringside one evening during the summer of 1934, in C. F. J. Park at Johnson City, where eight bouts were put on. He, his son, his nephew and the ladies of their families, were among the three thousand neighbors who enjoyed the spirited action. There were six events of three two-minute rounds and two principal bouts of five two-minute rounds—one of them as fast and clever as any I ever saw in Madison Square Garden. Like all men who know the game, George F. watched every move of the boxers with appreciation—and in silence. He was close to the ring, too, when eight bouts were held at En-Joie Park at Endicott, in the following week.

The East and the West branches give these amateur shows out of doors in alternate weeks during the summer, and in halls and armories through the winter—more than thirty exhibitions in the year. Five or six lads from the E. J. factories box at each show. The gate money is used to pay the expenses of contestants from other cities and to hire halls during the cold weather.

All the E. J. parks and most of the playgrounds are flooded when the first frost falls, and the workers and any others who care for the sport skate there through the season under the flood lights. Amateur championship meets are held there occasionally, and exhibitions by amateur and professional figure skaters.

Wherever an Endicott Johnson factory stands, surrounded by the homes of the workers, you will find not far away a playground for the workers' children. One of the first of these is C. F. J. Park at Johnson City, named in honor of the man who created it out of an unsightly mudhole. The three Johnson brothers, in 1913, bought a dozen acres, east of the Pioneer Factory, most of which had been stripped of clay by brickmakers and abandoned. The rest of it was an ash dump. C. Fred Johnson, in charge of Endicott Johnson building operations, drained the swamp, filled the old pond, and transformed the ancient eyesore into one of the beauty spots of the valley.

In a few months the gray waste became a pleasant expanse of green, with trees and flower beds, with a baseball diamond and tennis courts for the athletes, and swings, ladders and see-saws for the children. Close to it a deep artesian well was sunk, which supplies Johnson City with an unfailing flow of pure water from an underground river. When the diamond in C. F. J. Park could not accommodate the growing number of workers' teams, C. Fred laid out a new ball park for them a few blocks away, with cinder path and ground for track and field athletes, and a grand stand that seats five thousand spectators. Here regular matches of the New York-Pennsylvania league are played, and, in 1933, the field was equipped with flood lights, so that the workers and their neighbors can enjoy ball games and boxing matches in the cool of the evening.

Adjoining C. F. J. Park George F. Johnson built,

in 1926, one of the largest swimming pools in the country. It is an elevated structure of steel and concrete, with plenty of room for twenty-five hundred swimmers. The water, from an artesian well, renewed eight times a day, is filtered and warmed to summer temperature. The seventeen hundred lockers and dressing rooms, half of them for men and boys, the other half for women and girls, are completely modern. The pool is open from ten in the morning till ten at night. The price of a locker and a swim is ten cents. Children go in free during factory work hours. Life guards watch the swimmers. Back of the promenade at the edge of the pool are seats for spectators at exhibitions.

On the west side of Binghamton is a tract of some twenty acres, which George F. Johnson gave to the community in 1922, "under the one condition that it shall forever remain a public park." He suggested that in developing it the city should "carefully consider the recreational needs of mothers and children and emphasize the idea of holding family parties therein; that there shall be no fence along the street lines surrounding the park, and that its free use for innocent pleasure shall be unrestricted." The land cost $190,000, and Mr. Johnson gave $25,000 more for its improvement. There are tennis courts, an athletic field, baseball diamonds and a football field. Especial care has been taken to provide accommodations for mothers and babies and playground equipment for children, from sandpiles and swings to miniature outdoor gymnasium. The city officials wanted to name the place for the giver, but he persuaded them to call it Recreation Park.

Three thousand citizens of Binghamton gathered on a hill top in this park on Armistice Day, 1923, at the unveiling of a statue of George F. Johnson, erected by the people. Mr. and Mrs. Johnson and others of the family were present. His daughter, Mrs. Lillian Johnson Sweet, drew aside the drapery from a bronze group of heroic size, resting on a base of warm toned granite.

The central figure is a true likeness of Mr. Johnson, stalwart, well poised, forceful, the expression one of keen concentration and command, yet with a benign regard for a little girl, upon whose shoulder his right hand rests as she presents a spray of flowers. The figure is seated on a hide stretched over a work bench, and at the left side sits a robust worker, bare-armed and holding in his hand a shoe last, which he is studying intently. The attitude and the expression on the worker's face recall Rodin's Thinker. The two figures resting upon the same piece of leather symbolize the coöperation of labor and management in the upbuilding of a successful business and prosperous community. The inscription is: "George F. Johnson. Erected by an appreciative community to the nobility of his character and his great benefactions to the people."

Having read a list of George F. Johnson's gifts of $1,000,000, in 1922 alone, to the people of Broome County, I tried to compile a record of all he had given up to 1934, but could not get the details. "I don't think it would look nice to come out with a list like that," he said when I asked him. "The figures are scattered all around—don't think we could ever get them." From other sources I learned that the total is between $15,000,000 and $16,000,000.

En-Joie Park, near the Susquehanna river in Endicott, was a money-making resort until the Endicott Johnson company bought it, in 1916, and made it a workers' athletic field and playground. On two long, gently rolling hills are picnic grounds, with a pavilion containing a big dining hall and kitchen for holiday makers in case of rain. Scattered among the trees are tables of varying sizes to accommodate various groups.

There is a swimming pool, which two thousand bathers use on warm days; a wading pool for youngsters near it, and beyond that four tennis courts, all crowded from half-past four till dark. A merry-go-round provides free rides for all, and beside it is the free roller-skating rink, in what used to be the casino in the days when everybody paid. On the river bank is a boathouse and a fleet of rowboats.

Throughout the summer there is a free concert every Sunday evening in En-Joie Park by an excellent band of sixty-five pieces, with solos by noted singers and trumpeters, and an occasional quartette and chorus, artists all. Amplifiers carry the music clearly over half a mile. Camped on rugs from their cars, along grassy hillsides that curve around the band stand, are thousands of workers with their families, the smaller children running about. In the midst of the throng sit George F. Johnson and several members of his family. At the end of each number, the applause of the crowd is multiplied by the roar of hundreds of automobile horns in a weird Wagnerian chorus. The last triumphant crash of *The Stars and Stripes Forever* sends the audience home at nine o'clock, to be ready for work at seven Monday morning. It costs the E. J. company $30,000 a year to maintain En-Joie Park as a free playground.

One of the most popular recreational centres in the valley is George F. Pavilion, at the edge of C. F. J. Park, in Johnson City. It is a large modern structure of steel frame, with a suggestion of Spanish design in its architecture, and finished with tapestry brick and limestone. Mr. Johnson built it in 1926, as a good place to dance, and there has been dancing there three times a week ever since.

On this broad expanse of glassy floor twelve hundred couples can dance at one time. Seen by day, empty, it stretches away like a prairie, but on three evenings a week it is so crowded that the feeling of vast space is lost. Amplifiers carry the music to every corner of the ballroom, and on warm nights there are room and music to spare for dancing on the smooth tiling outside. Lawns and trees and beds of flowers surround the pavilion.

Friday evenings they have noted orchestras from out of town, and admission costs a dollar, and on Wednesday and Saturday evenings with twenty-five cents admission, first rate music, not quite so famous, is supplied. One Friday evening in 1934 I saw two thousand young men and women from all the E. J. factories from Binghamton to Owego gliding about the room in the newest dances. Occasionally a gray head appeared among the throng, and the older dancers seemed as happy as the rest. There were many visitors from Ithaca, Elmira, and Pennsylvania towns, and the scene was very like a college prom.

Some of the older workers wrote to George F., in the fall of 1934, asking why orchestras of national fame should be brought in at $1,000 a night, to take money out of the neighborhood. He replied, on the Workers' Page, that the workers were entitled to the best music, the company paid for it, and the entire gross receipts, some $60,000 a year were given to Broome County charities. Others wrote him, suggesting that the Pavilion would make an excellent gymnasium during the winter. The debate ceased when the E. J. Athletic Association leased the Binghamton State Armory and several other halls for four evenings a week, for the boxers and softball and basketball players.

There is a handsome merry-go-round in every one of the six playgrounds George F. Johnson has given to the children, from Binghamton to West Endicott. Each of them marks a step in his progress in getting even for the old days when he was lucky to ride a wooden camel once a year, and they all contribute to the happy life that helps a youngster to grow up into a strong and useful citizen. Mr. Johnson, in June, 1934, gave a merry-go-round to the children of North Side, Endicott, in the park his son George W. presented to the neighborhood. On the day it began to spin twelve hundred children, from four-year-olds to those of grammar school age, all freshly washed and brushed in their best clothes, marched past the tanneries and factories to George F.'s home, in Park Street.

Blowing horns, beating dishpans with long iron spoons, clashing saucepan lids for cymbals, whanging frying pans with pokers and rattling bits of brick in old kettles, the twelve hundred swarmed over the lawn while three little girls handed George F. a basket of flowers. His wife, his son and his nephew stood by. He was photographed with the flower girls and a small colored boy stood beside him.

"Let me tell you this," said George F. to the little army; "if anything has been done for you that has made you a bit happier, hand it on to somebody else, just as soon as you can. That's the way to keep square with the world. And now look. In that big park across the street there's a merry-go-round and ice cream. Help yourselves."

In a moment the lawn was empty of everything but a litter of tinware and old iron, on which lay two placards, scrawled with charcoal, "Our Three George F., George W. and Charley," and this bit of verse:

> When Your Here With Love We Greet You
> When Your Away With Grief We Grieve You

George F. was called to West Endicott playground a few days later, where six hundred youngsters clustered around him, and a small girl handed him a tall silver loving cup by way of thanking him for the new merry-go-round he had given them.

But everybody was not satisfied with the playground program. One worker wrote anonymously to George F., complaining that he'd rather pay ten cents a ride on a whip-go-round—a machine that breaks a rider's bones now and then—than ride free on a merry-go-round: besides, the company could make money on things like that. Mr. Johnson published the letter on the Workers' Page, with his reply that the company preferred to spend $30,000 a year on En-Joie Park, to provide innocent amusements free, rather than make it a "Bleeders' Park," with catch-penny devices. So many fathers and mothers wrote in to the same effect that the whip-go-round man was heard from no more.

When George F. heard, in the summer of 1934, that children from the south side of Johnson City were exposed to danger from traffic as they traveled across town to play in C. F. J. Park, he bought five acres on the south side and gave them to the community. Two thousand children, with banners and placards, turned out in a parade on the day he presented the deeds to the mayor, and joined their parents in cheering him. He told them that he would equip the playground as completely as all the others. He added: "I can see great things ahead for you little ones. I hope you will take advantage of all you have, and hand on every good thing to some one else."

On the way back to Endicott George W. remarked that the playground would be better if it could be made one hundred feet deeper—the baseball diamond needed more room between home plate and the centre field fence. Charles F., Jr. agreed with him. George F. said: "That sounds like a good idea. If we ought to have the ground, we can arrange to make an offer for it." Which was typical of his principle, never to be satisfied with anything if it could be made better.

But of all the good times George F. enjoys with his people, he and they seem to have the most fun at the clambakes and picnics. Informal, generally planned only a day or two in advance, they present the picture of an intimate relation between labor and capital that is unique. On a Saturday afternoon in late July, 1934, a dozen workers from the Sole Leather Tannery in Endicott unloaded a truck in the orchard of a little farm belonging to one of them. Some of the tanners drove stakes and on them set up a four-sided table in the shade. Others built an oven of stray bricks, started a fire and put bushels of hard clams to steam in a big caldron. When these were done, they put a few score of frankfurter sausages to boil in another caldron.

Still others rolled kegs of beer and ale within the table enclosure and set them beside many cases of bottled pop and soda. Three men carried in big cardboard boxes of sandwiches, while others tapped the kegs, drew beer in pitchers and passed the glasses. Wives and children of tanners sat in the family cars in the shade near by.

Into the orchard rolled two cars. In one sat George F., and his son, George W.; in the other C. Fred and his son, Charles F., Jr. Here were the Chairman of the Board, the President and the Vice President of the Endicott Johnson Corporation. They got out and walked in among the picnickers; shook hands here and there with old friends; nothing formal in the reception. They sat on benches where they happened to find empty places.

The younger tanners passed the food and the beer, beginning with the nearest men and giving the Johnsons theirs wherever they chanced to be. There sat George F., on the running board of a car, a sandwich in one hand and a glass of beer in the other, talking with a tanner about his little boy's liking for baseball. C. Fred was swapping jokes with an old-timer he hadn't seen all summer. Charley stood beside the table, eating clams out of the shell, listening with interest to a new tanner who was telling of his experiences in St. Louis and other shoe cities where he had worked.

When appetites were satisfied, a tanner with a violin and his small son with a guitar played accompaniment while the boy sang "The Spinning Wheel in the Valley" and other ballads. Two others in the party took a young pig out of a crate at the back of a car and smeared him from snout to tail with soapfat, put him back into the crate and carried him to the middle of the orchard. All hands stood in an irregular circle at twenty yards' distance.

"When you've been through the mill yourself," George F. remarked to me, "you can really join in the fun these lads have. Outsiders don't get the spirit of the thing. It's pretty hot here, and the beer will make them hotter, but they're having a fine time. Reminds me of the picnics we used to have when I was at the bench. A game of ball, shop against shop, with a keg of beer on third base. After a few innings every batter who hit the ball ran straight to third. Fight once in a while over a close decision, but no one was hurt—just part of the fun. I get around to most of these outings. They bring back old times and old fun."

When the crate was opened, the pig rambled a few steps, and as the crowd began to laugh and hoot, ran, doubled and slipped out of the reach of half a dozen tanners, who sprawled on the grass. A tall, tow-haired apprentice caught him at last and put him in the crate.

George W. Johnson stood near by, and the crowd gathered in the shade near him. "This pig," he said, "is now put up at auction, for the benefit of a worker who had the misfortune to hurt his arm pretty badly. How much am I bid? Who'll give a dollar?"

There were three or four bids of a dollar; then two, five, ten in quick succession. Charley offered twenty. His father raised it to fifty. "One hundred; make it a hundred," said George F.

"The pig is sold for one hundred fifty dollars as a starter," said the auctioneer—"George F.'s hundred and our fifty. And anyone who wants to add to it can chip in."

The young tanner who caught the pig took the bills from the Johnsons and smaller bills from the other workers. Then the Johnsons got into their cars and started for another picnic up Binghamton way.

The three chiefs—Charles F. Johnson, Jr., George F. Johnson, George W. Johnson

No fuss over their departure; just a lot of friendly goodbyes and waving hands.

Three clambakes in one day was George F.'s highest record in 1934, though on several days he attended two. They seem never to tire him, because they remind him of old times, and he enjoys being with his friends. His lively interest in everything they like is a fine tonic. That interest, as we have seen, includes field sports and athletic games as well as the picnics and other informal outings. In all of these there is a marked contrast with the idea underlying the athletic and other recreational activities promoted by the majority of employers. Many of them have baseball or football or hockey teams, whose triumphs make good advertising for the companies while the rest of the workers look on and cheer. But George F. Johnson's idea is to have sports and games for all, women as well as men, so that the greatest possible number can be healthier and happier.

A study of recreation in American industry reveals that, with a few isolated exceptions, employers began to provide games and other benefits for their workers under the stress of producing material for use in the World War. The demand was enormous. They stimulated their people not only with "pep" talks at noon but by furnishing baseball outfits and diamonds and many other amusements for off hours, all of which were good for their health and bettered their morale, thereby increasing efficiency.

It is difficult to understand why many leaders of industry began to lose sight of this valuable element in their business in the let-down after the war boom, but that is what happened.

Out of three hundred nineteen manufacturing companies, employing 1,309,802 workers, that replied to a questionnaire from the National Recreation Association in 1926, fifty-nine reported that they had athletic clubs for their people, one hundred fifty-seven provided fields and diamonds for two hundred thirty-three ball teams; fifty had tennis courts, forty-one promoted football or soccer, thirteen had golf courses, thirty-three had summer camps and one hundred seventy-seven gave annual picnics.

But since 1926 the extent of these activities, experts agree, has steadily dwindled, and since the depression of 1929 the falling off has been greater. This is in curious contrast with the Endicott Johnson sports program, which has reached its greatest development between the years 1929 and 1935. It is significant that the largest manufacturers of supplies for sports and games say that the employees of no other concern in America buy so much of their goods as the Endicott Johnson workers.

It is difficult to understand this contrast until one remembers that the Johnsons foster recreation because they like to have happy people—and they have the encouragement of finding that happiness reflected in more prosperity.

CHAPTER SIXTEEN

George F. Johnson—The Man and His Views

A FORCEFUL, kindly big man. That was my first impression of George F. Johnson when I met him during my visit to the valley in the summer of 1934. He was seventy-seven then, and looked fifty-seven. His glance searches you through, but it is friendly, and you feel at ease with him. His smile is cordial, and the grip of his hand is a welcome. It is a muscular hand, warm and powerful. His gray hair, close-cropped and vigorous, still shows splashes of red. His eyes are grayish blue, set well apart, and his ruddy cheeks, firm and well rounded, suggest the old athlete. The nose is aquiline, of medium length, the lips full but firmly closed, the mouth wide, with a humorous lift at the corners. The jaws are broad and deep, with an upward sweep to the rugged chin. It is the chin of a fighting man who goes through to the finish. The head is wide and round, forehead high; the neck full and muscular.

He is so broad of shoulder and full bodied that
he seems not much above medium height, until a
closer view reveals that he is only an inch or so below
six feet. His stalwart frame is well clothed with
flesh, big but not bulky, weight not much under two
hundred pounds. His speech is crisp, incisive, the
voice a baritone with a down-East tang. His robust
figure, his short, quick step and alert air, made me
think of a Yanke skipper on his quarter deck,
shrewd and genial, with the habit of command. There
is a certain vibrant quality about the man, hard to
define, a flow of energy that stimulates all who come
near him.

Mornings at seven George F. begins his day's
work, reading and answering letters in the office at
his home. By eight he is driving his roadster very
slowly through the streets of the towns, keen to discover where improvements may be needed, and waving his hand to children who hail him on their way
to school. He wears an old golf cap and a business
suit of quiet gray or brown. On his way he will drop
in at a factory or two, to see how the work is going.
Down the aisles he marches at a lively pace, keenly
on the watch, with a nod and a quick "Hello, Jim,"
to some old friend as he passes, but not stopping to
talk. Fault-finding trips, he calls these visits; not
that he utters a word of criticism, but he notices
things that might be bettered, and asks "the boys"
about them when he arrives in the office at nine.

The office is a plain, smallish room, not more than fifteen feet by twenty, separated by a wall of windows from the large main office of the Sole Leather Tannery at Endicott. A sensitive visitor asked him one day if he did not find the tannery odors unpleasant.

"No," he said. "They are sweet perfume to my nostrils; for when leather is being tanned, that means that we're going to make more shoes."

"The boys" are his son and his nephew, George W. and Charles F., Jr., president and vice president of the Endicott Johnson Corporation. George F. sits at his old roll-top desk, glances at a few memoranda, and swings around in an old swivel chair, to consult on the business of the day. The arms of that chair are deeply grooved where his son George tried out his new jack-knife on them thirty-odd years ago. George is full of responsibility now, middle-aged, with touches of gray on his dark temples. As George F. listens and talks, his elbows rest on the chair-arms, his finger tips touch. He leans back, physically at ease, but mentally concentrated on each problem that comes up, weighing every element in it, asking "the boys" for their judgment. He is about to speak—

A secretary taps at the door, and tells George F. that John Thompson wants to see him. He goes out quickly to where a worker in overalls is sitting on the reception bench. "Good morning, John," he says. "What's new with you?" John tells him what is on

his mind, and the two talk it over as any two old
friends might. "We'll look into it," says George F.
as he leaves his visitor. "I'll let you know." Ten seconds later he is back at the interrupted conference.
That finished, he is out driving his roadster again,
stopping now and then in some factory or laboratory.
No one ever knows when he will drop in. In the afternoon he and "the boys" confer again, at the office in
the old Pioneer Factory, Johnson City.

Perhaps he strolls for a few minutes over the fairways of the golf course, to see if anything needs to
be done, but not to play. It is a curious thing that this
man, who knows so well the value of play as a stimulus to better work, and helps all his employees to
play, himself never swings a club on the course he
built. There's a reason. "I get so damn mad at bad
shots," he says, "that it takes my mind off my business." He does his golfing down in Florida, where
he spends the four winter months; but even then he
keeps in close touch with the business. At En-Joie he
suggests improvements without forgetting business.

At the end of his day's work, George F. drives
back to Endicott at half-past four and puts away his
car. His home is sunny, spacious, plainly furnished,
with a quiet restful atmosphere in its large rooms.
Simplicity is the keynote of its comfortable, old-fashioned furnishings. He bathes, takes a nap for an hour,
puts on a fresh lounge suit, and comes down for a
look at the evening paper before dinner.

This is a simple meal, of things bought in the E. J. Workers' market. Mrs. Johnson, who has been busy all day with her girls' classes and the libraries, or calling on friends, is with him, and perhaps a few old neighbors. There is no formality, and there are seldom many guests. After dinner they talk a while and listen to some music. Ten o'clock is bedtime; for the next day begins at six.

Two or three times a week George F. and Mrs. Johnson attend dinners of the workers in one of the E. J. restaurants. Mr. and Mrs. George W. and Mr. and Mrs. Charles F., Junior are usually with them at the speakers' table. They all come in after the people are seated, and the diners greet them cordially, never with effusion, simply show they are glad to see their friends. There are many welcoming smiles and an outburst of handclapping as the Johnsons go to their places.

When George F. gets up to speak to the workers after dinner, no one would imagine that this sort of thing used to be an ordeal to him, but it was. In early days, when he knew every man and woman in the Pioneer Factory, it was a simple matter to talk with them face to face. But as the number of workers grew ten and twenty fold, this was impossible, and he had to address them in crowds or not at all. He had to learn the technique of public speaking, and he took on the new job and mastered it. He had the

great advantage of being familiar with his subject
and of knowing that he was among friends.

"Can you all hear me?" he begins. "Not much use
talking unless those farthest away can hear. You can
all hear? Good!"—and he's off. He hooks his left
thumb into the breast pocket of his coat, settles himself at ease, watches those in the back row, and pitches
his voice loud enough for them to hear without strain-
ing. His enunciation is clear, with a touch of New
England tang, and he emphasizes his points with a
thrust or a sweep of the right hand. The left stays
hooked to that breast pocket.

He talks to the workers in his usual homely, everyday phrases, with no attempt at oratory, like the ad-
vocate who wins his cause by discussing it as if he
were one of the jury. With this added advantage: his
hearers know from long experience that he is telling
them facts, and that what he advises is as much for
their benefit as his own. Whether he is paying tribute
to some worker who is being honored at the dinner,
or congratulating his people on good prospects
ahead, or warning them of a dull period coming,
his words ring with a vital force that carries con-
viction and calls out a salvo of applause. These cele-
brations and his attendance at the sports and picnics
of the workers are his diversions during the summer.
Whenever George F. and his workers get together,
they are apt to join in his favorite song, *Auld Lang
Syne*. At the great May Day celebration of 1934, in

his honor, every band that marched past the reviewing stand played it, and thousands of men and women
sang it as they saluted him.

Mr. Johnson's reading is devoted chiefly to magazines related to industry, especially his own. These,
with the Workers' Page, the daily newspapers and
an occasional biography or a novel, are his favorites.
He admires David Harum and similar stories of
local flavor. The model from whom Harum was
drawn, by the way, did business and swapped horses
in Binghamton. Sometimes, when he has read enough
for an evening, George F. drops in for a call on an
old chum and a brief chat about anything but business. "I'd rather have a bit of red herring and a glass
of beer with a friend," he says, "than the finest feast
in the world among strangers."

George F., his son and his nephew, work as a team
of three. George W. knows hides and leather as
thoroughly as Charles F., Jr. knows making and
selling shoes, and when the three meet, several times
a day, always within easy reach of the workers, they
have an intimate contact with the industry that no
absentee management can attain. That contact is
valuable, not only in stimulating production but in
straightening out any tangle that might occur.

And during Mr. Johnson's four months in Florida
the contact is not broken. Even though he is away,
the force of his directing genius is felt throughout
the industry and is an aid in its operation. Despite

his long absence every year, the business continues to prosper. The daily routine is controlled by the younger men, with greater authority and scope, but the triple conferences held daily go on just the same, thanks to the telephone. At the appointed hour George F. sits in at Seabreeze and each of "the boys" takes up a receiver in the home office, a thousand miles away, and for half an hour the three consult and plan and decide as if they were in the same room.

This supplements the correspondence that George F. keeps up every day by mail. If a problem of particular importance comes up, another call is put through, and the three talk it over at length. The chief keeps in touch with the social side of the organization, follows the fortunes of the individual members, by reading the Workers' Page every day. Letters to him from the workers and his replies to them appear on the page as regularly as if he were at home in Endicott. The spirit of their leader is always with them.

Seen in perspective, George F. Johnson's rise from a job at the bench to the head of an army of nineteen thousand tanners and shoemakers seems a reasonable, inevitable growth. Although opportunity did not present itself until he was past forty, he had been long preparing for it. His long look ahead, his great driving power, instinct for management and salesmanship have led to success. But the chief reason for this success has been the zeal of his employees. They work with him rather than for him, sure that they will get the highest pay besides their full share of the profits from their joint efforts.

That unique coöperation grows out of friendly understanding. He has no shop committee, to do at second hand what he does by direct contact; no company union, or labor representation on the board of directors, either of which, he believes, leads to suspicion and distrust. He has no rigid machinery for "welfare work;" never had any use for it. He helps his people to build homes, guards their health, provides for their comfort and recreation by sharing the cost with them—does it because he likes them and wants them to like him. They do.

Above all, he has given them security, steady work the year round, even in hard times, with better pay than other shoemakers receive. He takes care of the unfortunate and the aged. Fear for the future is unknown among Endicott Johnson workers.

All this is not the result of a scheme deliberately planned to produce profits. It has brought profits, but they have grown out of the united efforts of labor and capital working as partners. They have been and are united as the five brothers Rothschild in building for success. The keystone of the structure is the man's inborn genius for friendship. Nothing planned about that: it is spontaneous, has shown itself from boyhood, and always has been a powerful motive in all he has done.

He thinks of his organization as an industrial democracy, but it might be called a triumph of intelligent socialism. With this vital difference: Karl Marx urged labor to take capital by the throat and seize its rights; George F. Johnson has taken labor by the hand and led the way to their mutual welfare. True, he leads, but if any worker has a complaint he knows George F. is always eager to hear it. In all the twenty-nine factories there is no closed door between the worker and his chief. There is no grievance committee. Anyone who feels wronged can tell his story to George F. and be sure of a sympathetic hearing. Yet this is rarely needed; for the chances are that the man's director, or the next executive will straighten out the matter.

"The heart warm and the head cool," is George F.'s rule, and everyone in the organization has not only heard it but has often seen it in practice. Anyone who does not live up to it does not stay long in authority.

"The future is more important than the past," is another belief of George F.'s. With this in mind, he has organized his army of workers with a view to making it last. All promotions are made from the ranks, and he gradually gives men more power as they show their fitness to exercise it. Often when a man is taken from his machine and put in charge of a room, George F. publishes a letter to the workers, introducing him to them in his new capacity and asking for their loyal support. If — though this has seldom happened—the new director shows an arbitrary spirit, the superintendent of that particular factory asks him to be more considerate; and if that does not check him, he goes back to the ranks.

George F.'s son rose in this way to be president of the company, and his nephew to be vice president and general manager. Born in E. J. communities, they have always lived among the workers, played with them as boys and worked with them since they entered the business. For more than a decade they have shared the duties of management with George F., worked with him over business problems, joined him at the games and clambakes and entertainments of the men.

The workers speak of them as George W. and Charley. If they want to see either one on business, they call at the office; at other times they play ball or pitch horseshoes together without any feeling of restraint. The third generation of Johnsons are working in the factories, friends with their shopmates, and hoping to rise in their turn. If they deserve promotion, they will get it; if not, they won't: for George F. makes no exceptions to his cardinal principle— "the greatest good for the greatest number."

Can this democratic dynasty survive? So far as the second generation is concerned, it has been functioning for years and seems likely to go on. One thing that will carry it far is the tremendous impetus that

George F. has given it by many years of successful
operation. Another is the fact that it pays big profits,
not only in money but in the security and comfort and
happiness of all concerned. Mr. Johnson has never
pretended to be a prophet, yet he said to me as we
sat under the trees on his lawn one July evening in
1934:

"My boy George and Fred's boy Charley — we
three run the business now, and the boys have the idea
in their hearts as much as I have. When my time
comes to leave, they will carry on as we always have
—and I hope the generations after them will do the
same. This is a real industrial democracy — with
leadership, of course: no democracy can function
without leadership—and we hope to see it last a long
time.

"It will last as long as the leaders have in their
hearts that genuine love of the work and the workers.
Men reason with their minds—but they act from the
heart."

Charles F. Johnson, Jr., vice president in charge of
manufacturing, is confident that the system will continue. He said to me:

"So long as Mr. George F. is with us, we shall
go on as we have gone for years, growing and pros-
pering. I have never heard of any other employer
who has done, or even thought of doing, anything
like what he has done for the workers and for the
community. You have seen him among the workers,

and you know his warm friendship for them and their real affection for him. That solid friendship, that mutual regard, is the strongest thing in our organization.

"George W. and I hope our people will go on with us in the same way. And after us? Mr. George F.'s principles have been proved so right that I believe they are bound to prevail as long as this company lasts."

George F. Johnson's theory of industrial relations, evolved through decades of his leadership of a great enterprise, has proved its soundness by its success in practice. It works better than any other. So far as one can see, the prospects are that it will continue in practice indefinitely. The younger men have the principles at heart and live up to them, and at least nine-tenths of the workers live up to them, too. Every worker knows that he can rise to the top by proving his worth. George F. says there are men in the ranks able to run the industry. If all the Johnsons should retire—which is unthinkable—there would remain enough leaders to carry on the industrial democracy to success.

For the enterprise is to be carried on by more than a democratic dynasty, more than an industrial clan. The leaders have not only arisen from the ranks but they have been developed under the eye of the chief. In reality, George F. has brought down into modern times the old guild system, the master living in the midst of his business, with the homes of the workers next to his own and the homes of the sub-chiefs among them. Thus they are all in their daily lives, whether at work or at play, so closely interwoven that they are members of one family. Whoever shows the best qualifications for leadership is sure of recognition and promotion in this intimate association.

Whether the plan can be followed with advantage by American industry generally depends upon how genuinely the leaders adopt it. Half-hearted agreement will not do. All the externals may be there— good, cheap housing, medical care, recreation, provision for the aged,—but if the friendship back of them is lacking, they will not avail greatly. You can't fool all the people all the time.

George F. began by trying to make life happier for his companions, with no dream of the great industry he might create. He had lived in company houses in New England and hated them. From boyhood he had visioned the ideal factory, surrounded by the comfortable homes of the workers. In Binghamton, Lestershire and Endicott he saw his fellows living in cramped, unhealthy tenements, and as soon as he had money he began to help them to real homes. The development of medical care, establishment of playgrounds, athletics, libraries, classes in home-making, was a gradual growth.

The root of the plan was his friendship for his

When Labor meets Capital: George F. greets an old-timer from the tannery on the occasion of the May Day celebration in 1934

people. That he gathered harvests of profit from it was gratifying, but before that he had enjoyed the satisfaction of seeing his friends happy—which was his prime incentive. Governor Alfred E. Smith of the State of New York, expressed this in 1919, when he dedicated the Community Service House in Binghamton, to which the Johnsons had given $150,000. He said:

"There can come to the community that supports this house, there can come to George F. Johnson and the others who assisted so liberally, only what Divine Providence could wish for any man, for any community, because the work being done in this building and community is the work of the Divine Master himself."

Governor Nathan L. Miller said, at Binghamton, in 1922:

"There is here a common and mutual interest between employer and employee. I know of no other instance where such a perfect relation appears to have been established. Such complete success has been dependent upon the personality of one man and the confidence he has inspired.

"It appears to me that much of the confidence in Mr. Johnson on the part of his co-workers is due to the fact that they know him as one of them. He knows their problems; he knows what it means to earn his bread by the sweat of his brow; he realizes that to be truly happy one must work daily under the best conditions, must have confidence in his employer, must have pride in the work he is doing, and be assured of the future."

Speaking in 1916, to a big crowd in Binghamton in which there were thousands of Endicott Johnson workers, President Woodrow Wilson said:

"You are to be congratulated upon being connected with a company which considers its employees not alone as employees but as one big family.

"If the same spirit which exists between you and the members of the firm of Endicott Johnson and Company existed everywhere, there would be no question, no trouble, no difficulty as between the employer and the employee."

A president and two governors saw the whole situation clearly, and stated the essence of George F. Johnson's way of living: employers and employees one big family, having confidence in one another, pride in their work and earnest desire to help their neighbors. They saw the organization united as solidly as the Japanese people are united with their emperor, whom they revere as the descendant on earth of the sun goddess in the sky, while trusting him as their big brother, vitally concerned in the welfare of every one of them.

Mr. Johnson reflected the same idea when asked, in 1916, why he had come out for Wilson. "He is the only president I have studied," George F. said, "who has grasped the idea that a human being is more to be considered than dollars or a machine. I hold fast to the idea that human rights are greater than property rights. Wilson has fostered and pushed laws that give the average man a chance to rise in the world. His attitude toward public questions, and especially to social service measures, seems to me to be a very hopeful sign, not only for the country but for the world."

Every man's right to decent working and living conditions inspired Mr. Johnson to adopt, in 1916, the eight-hour day, far in advance of his competitors. He believes that improvement in methods and machines may well result in further shortening of the day's toil.

"Those who seek to maintain a ten-hour day or even a nine-hour day are wrong," he wrote in 1923. "I believe that within fifty years the six-hour day will be universally adopted." As to a thirty-hour week as an aid to economic welfare, the Endicott Johnson factories took a long step in that direction by operating on a schedule of five eight-hour days under the N R A. On that schedule wages still remained higher than in other shoe factories. When and if the thirty-hour week appears to be best for industry, it is safe to say that George F. Johnson will be among the first to adopt it, as he has been first in so many steps of progress.

George F. Johnson looks forward to wages constantly rising as labor and management constantly turn out better shoes at lower cost and in greater quantity. His ideal business is one in which every worker does his job so well that very little supervision is needed. After paying for costs and a fair return to capital, all surplus profit will be divided between labor and management, in equal shares for all, as it has been divided for years by the Endicott Johnson company. As efficiency advances, aided by every means within George F.'s power, workers will get their part—increased in value by the lower cost of housing, food and medical care in the communities.

Mr. Johnson and his brothers began to provide comfortable modern homes for their workers years before other manufacturers or the country at large gave much thought to the housing problem. In twenty years they have enabled their employees to buy two thousand houses at low cost, giving preference to those with the largest families. Their motive was to make life easier and happier for their partners in industry. Twenty years after they showed the way, governments and captains of industry have begun to worry over the housing situation.

George F. Johnson believes that if manufacturing corporations would help to make their workers comfortable in homes of their own, an important part of the national housing problem and of the industrial problem would be solved.

"My ideal," he says, "is the factory, with the home

of the owner near it, surrounded by the homes of the workers. His interests and theirs are the same. When they live pleasantly together, they will work together to better advantage than if they lived apart. When the owners are far away, their managers are tempted to make quick profits, regardless of how unjustly they may treat the workers. When all live as neighbors should, when workers and employers can talk over their troubles together, the troubles disappear. That is, if they are really friendly and know that each will prosper most by dealing fairly with the other. That sounds simple enough. It is simple. The best things in the world are simple.

"Sincere friendship is the foundation of coöperation. Without it, we get nowhere. With it, we can do our best for one another and for ourselves. No amount of charts and graphs, of planning, and scheming, can take the place of a square deal all round. Labor and capital must be friends if they are to succeed. And they can be friends best by being neighbors."

Mr. Johnson's aim has been to keep the business going, for the greatest good of all concerned, rather than to accumulate money. About the time it was incorporated, Mr. Endicott invited him to a meeting in New York, where a group of bankers offered to buy their company for $45,000,000. Mr. Endicott declared that he would be guided by what Mr. Johnson said. George F. read the proposition with care. "I say no," he decided. "There is not a single human note in it. It would destroy all we have built up."

Distinction outside of his business has no attraction for George F. Johnson. Before I had been very long in the valley I heard of movements that had been begun to send him to the United States Senate and to make him governor of the State of New York. I asked him what he thought of them.

"I have heard of those suggestions," he replied, "but I was never interested. I'm not a politician. My place is here, with my people and my business. I can accomplish something here that's worth while."

He was invited to Washington, in 1933, when the administration was conferring with industrial leaders on plans to organize the N R A, but he did not go.

"What would be the use of my going?" he said. "Politicians would only laugh at my ideas, say they were not practical. Anyone who wants to know can come here and see them in operation, live in the community, see and hear and feel how we all work and live together."

George F. has the good fortune to do things occasionally that attract the attention of the whole country. When industrial parades were being organized, in the spring of 1933, to signalize workers' and employers' approval of the N R A program, General Hugh L. Johnson telegraphed an invitation to George F. and his workers to join in the demonstration. Mr. Johnson replied that he was very sorry, but he and his people were all working eight hours a day and were too busy to parade. Those telegrams, reported by the Associated Press, made the front pages of most American newspapers.

In providing athletic sports for his people, George F.'s idea is that play is a necessary balance to work. More than half of his employees, women as well as men, play games all the year round. The principle is the same that a famous athletic coach expressed when I asked him what was the most important thing in turning out a winning team. I expected to hear some valuable technical details, but the coach said:

"Make your men comfortable; that's the great thing. See that they live in comfort, that they are properly equipped. Then you can work them hard today, and they'll turn out tomorrow, ready for more."

When he opened the En-Joie Health Golf Club, Mr. Johnson said, "Golf is just as good for the hard working shoemaker as it is for the tired business man. It refreshes him, makes him a better man."

Mr. Johnson's name was published, in December, 1934, among those who had million-dollar incomes before 1918. This was before the Endicott Johnson profit-sharing system was inaugurated, in 1919, and may have been one of his reasons for beginning it.

"Some people would feel honored," he declared to the E. J. workers. "The effect of such a publication on me is disgusting. I am ashamed and mortified.

Andrew Carnegie said, 'Any man who dies rich dies disgraced.' That is my sentiment.

"Any man who dies rich dies disgraced, especially in times like the present, when so many men, women and children are suffering for the common necessities of life. No man has a right, under such conditions, to pile up money. Every man and every woman has a duty to assist the needy, and the more they have or the faster they accumulate, the greater the duty."

Mr. Johnson recalled the years—"when everybody was making money and the country was on a huge drunk, so to speak, and millionaires were being made over night"—during which Mr. Endicott and he put all their profits into extending the business and building factories, which benefited the community. Then they made the partnership a corporation, and he received his share of the gains.

"From that time until the present," he continued, "my outgo has exceeded my income, until at the present time I have comparatively little left. It will be a source of satisfaction to you to know that each year my principal has dwindled, and my expenses, gifts and use of money, are increasing. Last year I think we dipped into the principal, to pay obligations of every kind, about $200,000. And, at the rate I am going, if I live five years, I shall probably be pretty near where I started—nil."

When men know the facts about any situation, Mr. Johnson believes, they will do the right thing. No one is more aware than he of the value of reliable publicity. For that reason he sends out some of the workers once in a while to see for themselves what conditions are in other shoe manufacturing communities. He pays their wages and traveling expenses to New England, New York and towns in the West where tanning and shoemaking are going on, so that they can judge how the others work and live and how they are paid. When the travelers come home they tell their friends what they have observed. They have never found any other place where the workers fare so well as in the E. J. communities.

As to the duty of employers to their employees, Mr. Johnson has this to say:

"In coöperation with labor, large industries should provide homes needed by workers, on a fair basis of interest charges, and sold at cost, with no profit.

"They should, if possible, operate a full and complete medical department, to take care of the health of workers and dependent members of their families. Thus coöperative medicine will be furnished them for half the cost if bought in open market. All these things are vitally important. . . .

"My conception of the true relation of labor and capital is for each industry—honestly capitalized, honestly organized and economically conducted—to pay its labor as much as possible, with a due regard for the rights of the investing and the consuming public.

"This would bring into control and for distribution an immense amount of capital now squandered by management in useless overhead, taking from labor and the consuming public both what fairly belongs to them, which, if given to them, would change the whole appearance of the picture as between labor and capital."

He told the ballplayers, to whom he gave $2,000 in prizes at their local World Series banquet in 1934, that "the finest thing about games is that in them we learn to give and take hard knocks. When the game is over, winners and losers shake hands, as good friends as ever. Many a Christian could take a lesson from athletes; learn how to fight fairly, for all he has in him, then take the result without either bragging or grumbling.

"Men and women who have enough good, healthy play are better citizens as a result of it. They enjoy life more than the sluggards; they are of more value to themselves and to the community. After a hard day's work, a game of ball or a round of golf or a swim make a fellow feel like a real man. Old-fashioned people are apt to forget that human beings need play as much as they need food to keep them at par. We have found that our workers not only enjoy their games but are more efficient because they play."

The philosophy underlying George F.'s gifts appears in a custom he began in 1905, and has kept up ever since.

"For a long time," he said, "Christmas was a sad day for me—to think of so many who had too much and of the great many who had nothing and felt worse on that day than on any other. Where could I find the people who were in the greatest need? In the jail, the almshouse, the orphan asylum and the old ladies' home."

So he took a big bag of ten-dollar gold pieces and set out on Christmas morning. He didn't preach or scold at the prisoners or ask them why they had gone wrong. He simply wished each one a Merry Christmas, shook his hand, left a gold piece in it and said, "This is no place for a man like you. I hope when I come here next year I shan't find you here."

One year two of George F.'s intimate friends disguised themselves as tramps, ragged and be-whiskered, and had the sheriff lock them in cells on Christmas morning. One of them was sobbing on his cot, but stood up when George F. asked what was the matter. Though the hobo kept his face half covered as he wiped away imaginary tears, George F. exclaimed, "Why, Bill, you damned old faker, here's your ten! Where's Rennie?" "In the next cell," said Bill. Rennie got his ten, too; for George F. was bound to carry out his design of giving, regardless of jokes.

After five years Mr. Johnson let his son, George, carry on for him; and George, after a while turned over the job to the Broome County Relief. Every year since then the prisoners and others have received their Christmas gifts, with George F.'s best wishes.

When the Community Chest plan was being promoted, in 1920, he invited eighty leaders in charity to dinner and persuaded them that the community did not want the plan. "It is a new idea, and people want to play with it a while," he said. "Let us stick to the old idea and give more. Don't get professional or mechanical. With the Community Chest, business houses would be assessed so much, just the same as taxes. It is unkind and un-Christian."

When a member of the clergy asked what religion had to do with the life of a manufacturer, Mr. Johnson said he assumed every man's life was part of a great plan.

"I believe," he continued, "that every worthy and good act in the life of a man is in accord with that plan; that service is real religion, and that real religion is found only in real service. It is just as much the part of a manufacturer to reveal his religion by service as it is for a minister of the Gospel. It must be looked for in the daily work of all men's lives."

At the same time he would have churches and all other institutions pay their way on a footing of equality. "One of the reasons this country is in a bad condition," he said, in 1933, "is that we have increased exemptions. We are going deeper and deeper into trouble because we are issuing millions of bonds exempt from taxation. I would not exempt church, school, or any other institution from taxation. All should come under a tax levy, and then your taxes would be about one-quarter to one-half of what they are today."

Humanity is George F. Johnson's religion. "All religions are good," he said to me, "and I believe in helping them all. I have never interfered with anyone's religious ideas. An employer can best show his religion to his workers by living up to it, by giving them a square deal and treating them as he'd like them to treat him."

When Mr. Johnson, in referring to his son, George W., said, "I saved George from college," he meant that he had saved him from wasting four years of the best time for learning his business by devoting it to studies which might not be helpful in his work.

"A boy who is going into professional life," he says, "must go to college as a preparation for his technical training; but the average boy who is going into business had better begin to learn that business as soon as he finishes in a good secondary school."

We have seen in these pages what George F. Johnson is, what are the motives that impelled him, and how he has established and developed an industrial democracy that is unique in the history of our times. The friendship between him and his people has endured unbroken for nearly forty years, unbroken under the strains of hard times and the temptations of prosperity. It is a phenomenon that challenges attention.

Beginning at a time when the worker's attitude toward his employer was one of suspicion and downright hostility, when generations of harsh treatment and strife had brought both parties in the world of industry into a state of chronic distrust, Mr. Johnson has gone steadily forward on his course, winning and holding the friendship of his people, and quite as steadily extending his business and increasing the prosperity of his company. There have been, of course, times of discouragement, but in those times George F. has taken a fresh grip on his job, cheered by the line he often quotes, from St. Paul's letter to the Galatians: "Be not weary in well doing, for in due season ye shall reap if ye faint not."

THE END